Egg marketing

A guide for the production and sale of eggs

FAO
AGRICULTURAL
SERVICES
BULLETIN
150

FOOD AND AGRICULTURE ORGANIZATION OF THE UNITED NATIONS
Rome 2003

The designations employed and the presentation of material in this information product do not imply the expression of any opinion whatsoever on the part of the Food and Agriculture Organization of the United Nations concerning the legal status of any country, territory, city or area or of its authorities, or concerning the delimitation of its frontiers or boundaries.

ISBN 92-5-104932-7

Preface

This guide provides information and advice to those concerned with the production and sale of eggs in developing countries with an emphasis on marketing, i.e. producing in order to meet market demand. Market-led egg production enables long-term business survival, higher profits and a better standard of living for the egg producer.

Improvement measures discussed in this publication have been found to be effective in practice. However, as is inevitable with any publication attempting to address such a wide range of conditions, some of the recommendations and observations found herein may be unsuitable to the reader's particular circumstances. The reader should select what appears advantageous for the solution of his or her own particular problem(s).

This publication is based upon and updates the FAO Marketing Guide No. 4, *Marketing eggs and poultry* by J.C. Abbott and G.F. Stewart, first published in 1961. It has been prepared by Edward S. Seidler, Senior Officer (Marketing), AGSF, and Martin Hilmi who worked in FAO under FAO's Volunteer Programme. Simon Mack and Emmanuelle Guerne Bleich of FAO's Animal Production Service (AGAP) provided technical advice on poultry production issues and commented on various drafts of this guide.

Contents

Preface iii
Introduction ix

Chapter 1
EGG PRODUCTION **1**
Production 1
Egg production cycle 10
Production costs and profits 16

Chapter 2
MARKETING QUALITY EGGS **29**
Quality criteria 29
Quality maintenance 35
Grading and standardization 41

Chapter 3
EGG PACKAGING, TRANSPORT AND STORAGE **53**
Packaging of shell eggs 53
Storage of eggs 57
Transport of eggs 63

Chapter 4
MARKETING ORGANIZATION FOR EGGS **67**
Direct marketing 68
Marketing channels 69
Marketing intermediaries 70
Evaluation of the marketing channel 72

Contents, continued

Chapter 5
PRICING AND SALES POLICY   73
    Demand and supply   73
    Pricing   73
    Development of sales outlets   78

Chapter 6
MARKETING SERVICES   81
    Extension and training   81
    Market information services   84
    Marketing research   86
    Programmes to expand consumption   88
    Trade associations   89
    Credit   89

Chapter 7
LIVE BIRD MARKETING   91
    Quality criteria   91
    Processing   96
    Marketing organization for live birds   97

    References   101
    Photographs   105

Figures

1   Lighting schedule   8
2   Temperature and its effects on egg production   9
3   Percentage of productive laying flock over a period of time   13
4   Number of eggs produced over a period of time   14
5   Gross output and factors affecting the profitability
        of an egg enterprise   20
6   Egg composition   30
7   Egg weight increase over a period of time   31
8   Evaporation cooling in dry climates   39
9   Interior quality of eggs by United States standards   45
10 Side view for egg quality   47
11 Layout of packaging and storage facility   61
12 Direct marketing   67
13 Organized marketing channel   68

Tables

1   Types of poultry enterprises   1
2   Production schedule in temperate climate   12
3   Production planning   15
4   Expenses for rearing   17
5   Weekly costs and sales   17
6   Costs and income for a production cycle   19
7   Summary of United States grade standards
        for individual shell eggs   42
8   Recommended temperatures for loading and transport   64
9   Marketing costs   75
10 Total costs   76

Introduction

Augmenting the production of laying chickens is an important objective in helping to meet the nutritional needs of growing populations in developing countries. These chickens are prolific, easy to raise and their output can be generally expanded more rapidly and easily than that of other livestock. Furthermore, they are adaptable to various climates and altitudes. Poultry raising can often be combined with other types of farming and offers the possibility to raise extra revenue for farmers.

The land and capital requirements to start a small enterprise are not great, yet farmers who market eggs on a regular basis have a valuable source of ready cash. Eggs provide an inexpensive and valuable source of nourishment. Weight for weight, an egg contains about the same amount of animal protein as pork and poultry meat, about three-quarters that of beef and two-thirds that of whole milk cheese.

Eggs are an important and fundamental foodstuff for developing countries. It is not sufficient, however, to produce supplies at a reasonable cost. Arrangements must be made to ensure that the eggs reach the consumers. With increasing urbanization, eggs will need to be assembled, packed and transported in good condition to distant cities and distributed through retail outlets conveniently situated near consumers.

The tasks involved in marketing eggs are:

- collecting;
- grading and packaging on farm or transporting to a grading, packaging and processing plant;
- storing;
- moving through wholesale and retail channels; and
- selling directly to consumers.

Before new or improved marketing methods are introduced, an accurate survey of current industry conditions should be made, and an understanding of production and consumption patterns and factors that have determined these should be developed. Marketing improvement programmes may range in their objectives from relatively simple changes in handling and packaging methods to a reorganization of the marketing channels. Frequently, important marketing improvements can be effected simply by correcting specific handling, transport, packaging, grading and storing methods. Efficient marketing must satisfy consumers' demands and preferences.

Chapter 1
Egg production

PRODUCTION

Poultry enterprises may vary from basic backyard poultry keeping to mechanized and automated production plants. Various types of poultry enterprises are illustrated in Table 1.

Table 1
Types of poultry enterprises

	Backyard poultry	**Farm flock**	**Commercial poultry farm**	**Specialized egg production**	**Integrated egg production**
Subdivision of egg production	Pullet growing, feed production	Hatchery production separate from farming	Feed production separate from poultry farms	Chicken meat production becomes independent of egg production	Separate enterprises reintegrated as a business
Main management characteristics	Natural hatching	Artificial hatching and sexing	Feed mixing	Egg processing plant	Controlled-environment houses
Type of farming	Subsistence farming	Mixed farming	Joint egg and meat production	Eggs industry (single commodity)	Egg complex
Labour	Part-time	Part-time	Full-time	Division of management and labour	Separate daily work and random work
Building	Free range	Water feeder	Water feeder	Manure disposal equipment	Egg belt automatically controlled house

Backyard poultry production is at the subsistence level of farming. Birds live free range and hatch their own eggs. Their diet is supplemented with crop waste or food leftovers. The labour involved in backyard poultry production is part-time.

Farm flock production is slightly more specialized. Eggs are hatched at a separate location where the hatch and the sexing of the birds are controlled.

Commercial poultry farm production involves full-time labour and is geared toward producing on a sufficient scale for the sale of both eggs and poultry meat.

Specialized egg production consists of separating poultry for meat and egg production. In the egg producing plant, specialized employees oversee specific aspects of egg production.

Integrated egg production is the most advanced enterprise and involves full mechanization and automation of the egg production cycle including battery egg laying, temperature controls, scientific feeding and mechanized egg collection methods.

Types of brooders

Basket brooder

Oil barrel – charcoal

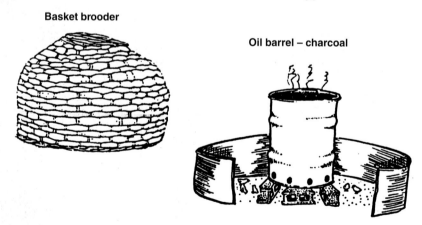

Source: Reid et al., 1990

All of the above poultry-keeping methods are used in the developing world, but the majority of the enterprises are backyard poultry and farm flock production. The poultry and egg sectors are highly fragmented. Most of the production is carried out by a large number of farmers, each with a very small flock. The greater part of produce is sold in markets close to the farms.

Day-old chicks are usually obtained from local hatcheries licensed by international hybrid breeding companies. Farmers or cooperatives of farmers may choose between varieties of chickens for egg production and meat production.

The small chicks can be either naturally or artificially brooded. If artificially brooded, small chicks must be placed in a separate house from laying chickens and it is necessary to protect the chicks from predators, diseases and catching colds. This stage of brooding lasts for eight weeks. In the first four weeks of life, small chicks need to be housed in a brooding box. Some typical types of brooders are shown below and on the previous page.

Kerosene brooder

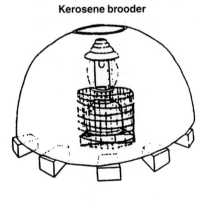

Storm lantern brooder

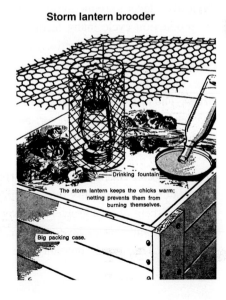

Drinking fountain

The storm lantern keeps the chicks warm; netting prevents them from burning themselves.

Big packing case.

After the first month, small chicks are removed from the brooder box and placed in the brooder house. At two months of age, the chicks enter the grower stage which lasts until they are five months (20 weeks) old. Growers may either be housed separately from small chicks or continue to be reared in brooder-cum-grower houses. It is important to properly manage the growers as their reproductive organs develop during this period and this will affect their egg production capacity in the future.

When the growers reach 18 weeks of age they are moved to laying houses and begin to lay eggs, which are, however, small and unmarketable. It is not until they are 21 weeks old that the growers reach their commercial laying stage. Layers may be placed in intensive, semi-intensive or free-range types of housing.

The choice of housing is determined by climate, type of production desired and the farmer's financial resources. Some examples of laying houses are shown on the next two pages.

Photographs 1 through 5 (see photograph section) are other examples of laying houses.

Factors affecting egg production

Typically, a layer's production cycle lasts just over a year (52-56 weeks). During the production cycle many factors influence egg production; therefore, the cycle must be managed effectively and efficiently in order to provide maximum output and profitability. The following factors influence egg production.

Breed. The breed of the laying bird influences egg production. Management and feeding practices, however, are the key determining features for egg production.

Mortality rate. Mortality rate may rise due to disease, predation or high temperature. The mortality rate of small chicks (up to eight weeks of age) is about 4 percent; that of growers (between eight and 20 weeks of age) is about 15 percent; and that of layers (between 20 and 72 weeks of age) is about 12 percent. The average mortality rate of a flock is from 20 to 25 percent per year.

Types of laying houses

Housing for hot – arid climates

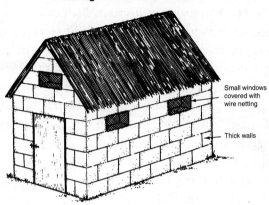

Small windows covered with wire netting

Thick walls

Open-house type

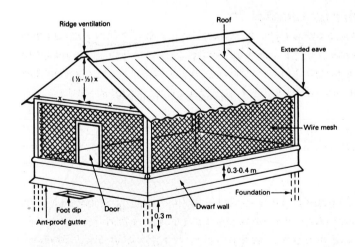

Ridge ventilation

Roof

Extended eave

(½ - ⅓) x

Wire mesh

0.3-0.4 m

Foundation

Foot dip

Door

Dwarf wall

Ant-proof gutter

0.3 m

Sources: Kekeocha, 1985; Oluyemi and Roberts, 1979

Types of laying houses, continued

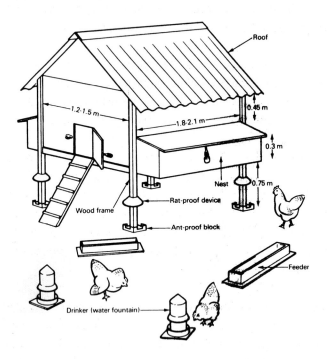

Moveable type housing

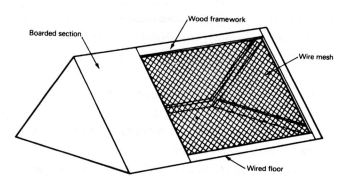

Age. Birds typically begin producing eggs in their twentieth or twenty-first week and continue for slightly over a year. This is the best laying period and eggs tend to increase in size until the end of the egg production cycle.

Body weight. In general, optimum body weight during the laying period should be around 1.5 kg, although this varies according to breed. Underweight as well as overweight birds lay eggs at a lower rate. Proper management and the correct amount of feed are necessary in order to achieve optimum body weight.

Laying house. The laying house should be built according to local climatic conditions and the farmer's finances. A good house protects laying birds from theft, predation, direct sunlight, rain, excessive wind, heat and cold, as well as sudden changes in temperature and excessive dust. If the climate is hot and humid, for example, the use of an open house construction will enable ventilation. The inside of the house should be arranged so that it requires minimum labour and time to care for the birds.

Lighting schedule. Egg production is stimulated by daylight; therefore, as the days grow longer production increases. In open houses, found commonly in the tropics, artificial lighting may be used to increase the laying period. When darkness falls artificial lighting can be introduced for two to three hours, which may increase egg production by 20 to 30 percent.

In closed houses, where layers are not exposed to natural light, the length of the artificial day should be increased either in one step, or in a number of steps until the artificial day reaches 16 to 17 hours, which will ensure constant and maximized egg production. Effective day length should never decrease during the laying period. An ideal artificial light schedule is shown in Figure 1.

Feed. Free-range hens will produce more meat and eggs with supplemental feed, but only if they are improved breeds or crossbreeds. The selection of local hens is done on the basis of resistance and other criteria rather than feed utilisation for production.

Fresh and clean water should always be provided, as a layer can consume up to one-quarter of a litre a day.

Figure 1
Lighting schedule

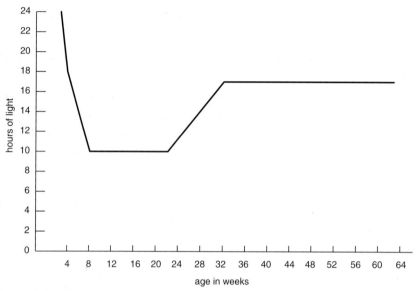

Source: Smith, 1990

Culling. Culling is the removal of undesirable (sick and/or unproductive) birds, from the flock. There are two methods of culling:

* mass culling, when the entire flock is removed and replaced at the end of the laying cycle; and
* selective culling, when the farmer removes individual unproductive or sick birds.

Culling enables a high level of egg production to be maintained, prevents feed waste on unproductive birds and may avert the spreading of diseases.

Climate. The optimal laying temperature is between 11° and 26° C. A humidity level above 75 percent will cause a reduction in egg laying. Figure 2 indicates the effect temperature has on egg production.

Figure 2
Temperature and its effects on egg production

Temperature (°C)	Effects
11 – 26	Good production.
26 – 28	Some reduction in feed intake.
28 – 32	Feed consumption reduced and water intake increased; eggs of reduced size and thin shell.
32 – 35	Slight panting.
35 – 40	Heat prostration sets in, measures to cool the house must be taken.
40 and above	Mortality due to heat stress.

Source: Kekeocha, 1985.

When the temperature rises above 28° C the production and quality of eggs decrease. Seasonal temperature increases can reduce egg production by about 10 percent.

Management factors. Effective and efficient management techniques are necessary to increase the productivity of the birds and consequently increase income. This entails not only proper housing and feeding, but also careful rearing and good treatment of the birds.

Vaccination and disease control. Diseases and parasites can cause losses in egg production.

Some of the diseases are as follows:

- bacterial: tuberculosis, fowl typhoid
- viral: Newcastle, fowl plague
- fungal: aspergillosis
- protozoan: coccidiosis
- nutritional: rickets, perosis

Some of the parasites are:

- external: lice, mites
- internal: roundworms, tapeworms

Vaccinations are administered to birds by injection, water intake, eye drops and spraying. Clean and hygienic living quarters and surroundings may eliminate up to 90 percent of all disease occurrences.

Collection of eggs
Frequent egg collection will prevent hens from brooding eggs or trying to eat them and will also prevent the eggs from becoming damaged or dirty.

EGG PRODUCTION CYCLE
Birds usually start to lay at around five months (20-21 weeks) of age and continue to lay for 12 months (52 weeks) on average, laying fewer eggs as they near the moulting period.

The typical production cycle lasts about 17 months (72 weeks) and involves three distinct phases, as follows.

- *Phase 1: Small chicks or brooders.* This phase lasts from 0 to 2 months (0-8 weeks) during which time small chicks are kept in facilities (brooder houses) separate from laying birds.
- *Phase 2: Growers.* This phase lasts about 3 months, from the ninth to the twentieth week of age. Growers may be either housed separately from small chicks or continue to be reared in brooder-cum-grower houses. It is

important to provide appropriate care to the growers particularly between their seventeenth and twentieth week of age as their reproductive organs develop during this period.

- ***Phase 3: Layers.*** Growers are transferred from the grower house to the layer house when they are 18 weeks old to prepare for the laying cycle. Birds typically lay for a twelve-month period starting when they are about 21 weeks old and lasting until they are about 72 weeks old.

Production planning

On average a bird produces one egg per day. Furthermore, not all birds start to lay exactly when they are 21 weeks old. Planning is therefore required for egg production to be constant so as to meet market demand. A schedule similar to the one shown in Table 2, which indicates on average satisfactory levels of production for a flock of birds, can be used.

In areas where the climate is hot and humid, commercial hybrid laying birds produce on average between 180 and 200 eggs per year. In more temperate climates birds can produce on average between 250 and 300 eggs per year. The table below illustrates a typical production schedule in a hot and humid climate.

In Table 2 the age of the flock is shown in the first column and the percentage of birds that actually lay during that week of age is shown in the second column. Usually at 21 weeks of age only 5 percent of the flock lay.

As shown in the third column, for 100 birds at 21 weeks of age only five would actually be laying. In the fourth column the actual number of eggs produced is shown. On average a bird produces 208 eggs over a twelve-month period, which is a weekly production rate of four eggs per bird. At 21 weeks of age 20 eggs are produced (five birds produce four eggs each) and at 22 weeks 40 eggs are produced, etc.

The graph in Figure 3 shows the actual percentage of productive laying flock over a period of time, and the graph in Figure 4 shows the number of eggs produced over a period of time for 100 birds. Egg production rises rapidly and then starts to fall after 31 weeks of age. When less than 65 percent of the flock are laying eggs (71 weeks of age), it may become uneconomical to retain birds. Feed costs and sales of culled birds for meat must be considered as well

Table 2
Production schedule in temperate climate (100 birds)

Age of flock (in weeks)	% of flock laying	No. of birds laying	No. of eggs produced per week
21	5	5	20
22	10	10	40
23	18	18	72
24	34	34	136
25	52	52	208
26	65	65	260
27	74	74	296
28	84	84	336
29	88	88	352
30	92	92	368
31	94	94	376
32 - 39	88	88	352
40 - 47	83	83	332
48 - 59	77	77	308
60 - 64	73	73	292
65 - 70	70	70	280
71 - 76	65	65	260

as prices for eggs. In some instances when egg prices are high it may be viable to delay culling birds until only 45 percent of the flock is still laying eggs (78 weeks of age).

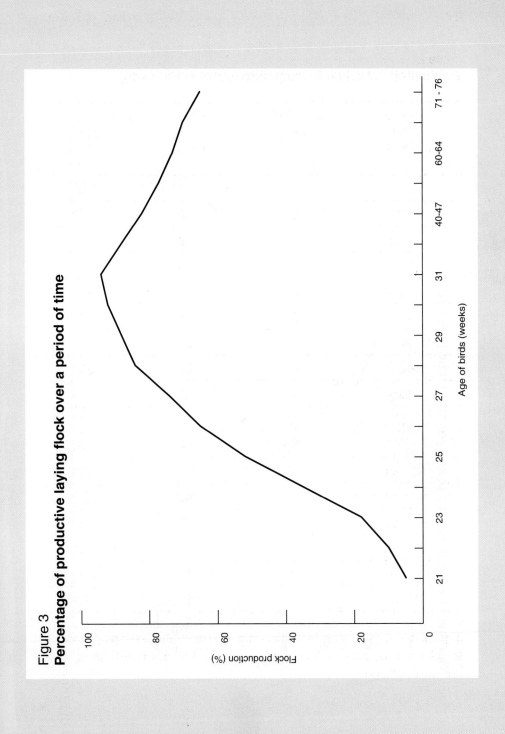

Figure 3
Percentage of productive laying flock over a period of time

Figure 4
Number of eggs produced over a period of time (100 birds)

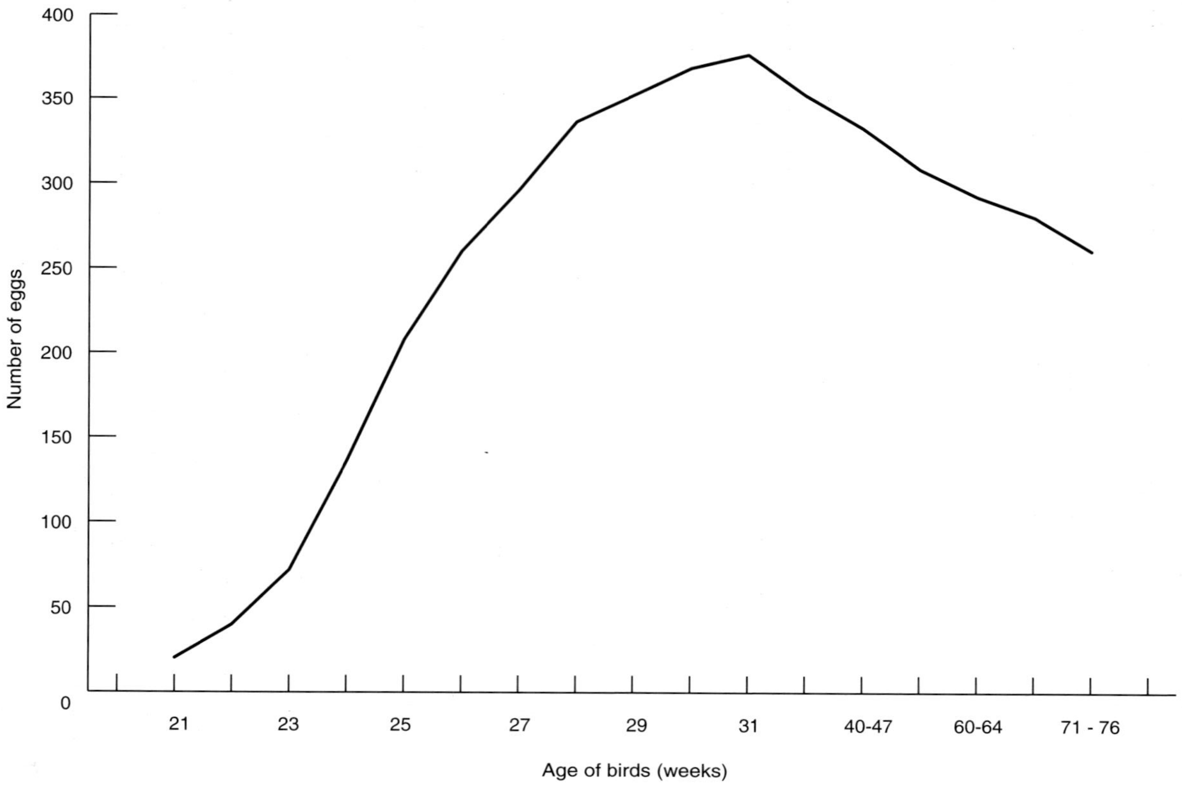

Clearly, egg production requires planning for costs as well as for profit generation and for meeting market demand. Planning involves not only the number of eggs laid by the flock over a period of time, but also when to hatch chicks to replace birds with diminishing laying capacity.

If production is to be kept constant, a simple chart as shown in Table 3, for example, will be needed to plan when new chicks must be hatched so that they can be introduced to laying in time to pick up on diminishing egg production.

Table 3
Production planning

Layer flocks	0	11	21	31	41	51	61	71	81
	(...................... time in weeks ....)								
1st layers	Born		Lay						
2nd layers			Born		Lay				
3rd layers				Born		Lay			

As indicated on the chart, the first layer flock was hatched at 0 weeks to become productive after 21 weeks. The second flock of layers was hatched at the 21st week to be ready to lay after the 41st week, as the first layer flock starts to diminish production. This type of production entails having flocks of birds of different age groups.

Clean and hygienic living quarters and surroundings are essential to control disease. There should be no more than three or four different flock age groups present at one time. The mortality rate on average is between 20 and 25 percent. This means that if one wants 100 birds to lay, it may be necessary to buy between 120 and 125 small chicks.

PRODUCTION COSTS AND PROFITS

Records should be kept of costs incurred during the operation and of proceeds from the sale of eggs. Costs must be covered by the sales of eggs. The difference between the proceeds from the sales and costs incurred represents profit.

Brooder-grower stage

The costs to be considered are not only those concerned with the birds during the laying period, but also those incurred in the brooder and grower stage during which time no eggs are being produced. The brooder-cum-grower stage lasts about five months (0-20 weeks). The main costs to consider during this stage can be seen in Table 4.

Laying birds

Once the costs for the brooder-cum-grower stage have been calculated, it will be possible to calculate costs for the laying birds. Calculations may be made on a daily, weekly or monthly basis. However, the most useful calculations are made at the end of the laying cycle. Daily, weekly or monthly calculations give approximate indications of costs and relative profits or losses. The main concern for farmers during this period is probably whether or not the proceeds from the sale of eggs cover feed and rearing costs. Feed cost is generally estimated to be about 75 percent of the production cost of eggs.

Comparing feed and rearing costs and egg proceeds for a week or a month may give an indication of profitability or loss. A farmer would have to subtract the cost of feed for a week from the proceeds for the total number of eggs sold that week. Furthermore, the rearing costs (expenses incurred before the birds start laying) should be amortized. This can be calculated by dividing the total rearing costs by the laying period. If rearing costs are US$ 10 and the laying period is 52 weeks, cost per week for rearing is US$ 0.19. Table 5 shows a simple record of weekly costs and sales.

Costs and income for the laying cycle

Calculations for the laying cycle (52 weeks) are more accurate and enable the farmer to determine whether the egg laying enterprise is running at a profit or a loss.

Table 4
Expenses for rearing

Costs	US$
Chicks (total number of chicks multiplied by price per chick)	
Feed (total kg of feed multiplied by price per kg)	
Housing	
Equipment	
Labour	
Vaccinations	
Mortality	
Loan	
Various	
Total costs	

Table 5
Weekly costs and sales

	US$
a) Eggs sold	
b) Feed used	
c) Rearing costs	
a minus b and c =	

Costs. When calculating costs for the laying cycle, the main expenditures to consider are:

- rearing – rearing brooders until they become layers;
- housing – building or maintaining laying house and brooder house;
- equipment – the cost of miscellaneous items such as feeders, buckets, etc.;
- feed – total feed used during the year;
- labour – labour costs incurred to manage birds;
- vaccinations – medicines and veterinary visits;
- mortality – loss of laying birds due to disease, etc.; and
- various expenses – lighting, water, etc.

Income. When calculating income for the laying cycle, the earnings to consider derive from:

- the sale of eggs;
- the sale of culled birds after the first cycle of production; and
- where applicable, manure sold as fertilizer.

Table 6 shows an example of record keeping for yearly production costs and income.

Initially, capital is required to start an enterprise; proceeds from the sales of eggs should, however, provide funds to continue with the business before the end of the first laying cycle. Indeed, three months after point of lay (30 - 31 weeks of age), when the birds should normally have reached peak production, the proceeds from the sale of eggs should be sufficient to operate the business on a revolving fund basis. The three-month period is sufficiently long even for the low producing birds or those that peak late.

Figure 5 shows the various factors that affect the profitability of an egg enterprise.

Table 6
Costs and income for a production cycle*

Costs	US$
Rearing (carried forward from table 4)	
Houses	
Equipment	
Feed	
Labour	
Vaccinations	
Mortality	
Various expenses	
Total costs	
Income	
Sale of eggs	
Sale of culled birds	
(Sale of manure)	
Total income	
Profit	

*This table does not include marketing costs (see Chapter 5, Pricing and sales policy).

Figure 5

Gross output and factors affecting the profitability of an egg enterprise*

*Gross output and factors affecting the profilablifty of an egg enterprise**

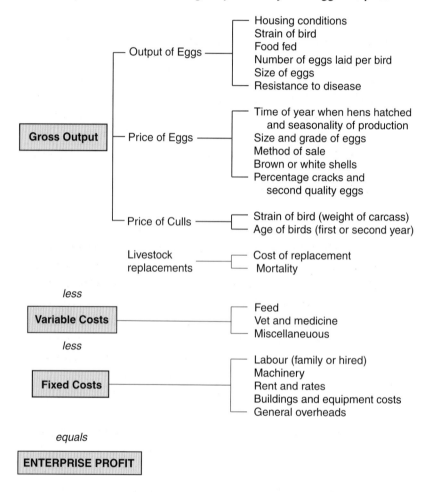

Gross Output

Output of Eggs
- Housing conditions
- Strain of bird
- Food fed
- Number of eggs laid per bird
- Size of eggs
- Resistance to disease

Price of Eggs
- Time of year when hens hatched and seasonality of production
- Size and grade of eggs
- Method of sale
- Brown or white shells
- Percentage cracks and second quality eggs

Price of Culls
- Strain of bird (weight of carcass)
- Age of birds (first or second year)

Livestock replacements
- Cost of replacement
- Mortality

less

Variable Costs
- Feed
- Vet and medicine
- Miscellaneuous

less

Fixed Costs
- Labour (family or hired)
- Machinery
- Rent and rates
- Buildings and equipment costs
- General overheads

equals

ENTERPRISE PROFIT

*Draft FarmManagement Training Manual, AGSF, Rome, 2002.

The following guidelines have been selected from the FAO Special Programme for Food Security (SPFS) Diversification Component, May 1997.

Guidelines for improved household poultry production

Constraints. The main limitation to improved household poultry production is the extremely high loss of birds before they reach maturity caused by inadequate nutrition and disease. This loss means that a high proportion of all the eggs laid have to be kept for replacement stock leaving little, if any, surplus for sale or consumption.

The main causes of loss are:

- **Poor nutrition** is the major cause of loss and predisposes birds to disease, poor immune response to vaccines and predation.
- **Disease,** especially the highly infectious viral Newcastle Disease (ND), which is believed to be endemic in most rural flocks. Clinically the disease is cyclic and occurs at times of climatic and nutritional stress. The virulent (velogenic) strain common in Africa and Asia can, but not always, cause up to 80 percent mortality in unvaccinated chickens. Fowl cholera (pasteurellosis), coccidiosis, Gumboro disease (infectious Bursal disease) and fowl pox can also, to a lesser extent, cause problems in rural flocks.

Poor, or non-existent housing, is also a major cause of high losses. Without being able to confine birds at night, it is almost impossible to catch and vaccinate them, although new types of ND vaccine can be administered in the feed. Shelter can also provide protection for young birds against predators and can ensure that all the eggs are laid in the proper place and not lost.

The majority of indigenous breeds or strains of chicken/fowl have evolved to survive under harsh conditions where they largely have to fend for themselves. Such hardiness, however, is at the expense of higher levels of productivity and they are less able to exploit the advantages of improved management, nutrition, etc., than breeds with a greater genetic potential for egg production and feed conversion (growth).

Potential. Improved management and disease control can have a substantial impact on household economies. Under traditional management the majority of eggs are hatched to ensure sufficient replacements with only the male birds being sold or consumed. Reduced losses will ensure that more birds could be successfully reared and, assuming the extra birds can be properly fed, this will allow more eggs to be collected and consumed or sold as a regular source of income.

Potential interventions
The basis for any improvement programme will be improved husbandry, notably housing, nutrition and disease control, primarily Newcastle Disease. Subsequent interventions would concentrate on further improving nutrition and the introduction of improved breeds/strains.

Improved feeding. Most household flocks rely on scavenging and household scraps and, depending on conditions, this is usually adequate for survival and a low level of production. However, inadequate nutrition, exacerbated by marked seasonal fluctuations, is a major predisposing factor to disease and high mortality. As investments are made in improved animal health, housing and, especially if improved birds are to be introduced, then attention must be given to diet supplementation or feeding a complete diet in the case of totally confined birds.

Conventional feed materials such as maize, wheat, barley, oilcakes, fishmeal, etc., are rarely available to the back-yard producer. In many developing countries these are in short supply and even compounded feeds may be of dubious quality. For household production systems, however, there are usually a wide range of locally available feedstuffs that can be used in addition to household scraps. These include: surplus/broken or second grade grains (cereals, maize, sorghum and millet); roots and tubers (sweet potatoes, cassava, etc.), green material (legumes and leaf meals, sweet potato vines, etc.), residues and agro-industrial by-products (bran, rice polishings, oilseed cakes, etc.). Unless a complete balanced ration is available, the ability to free range is important to allow the birds to feed on insects and worms, green material, etc., so that they can balance their essential amino acids, mineral, vitamin, as well as energy requirements. Where appropriate, improved feeding systems (troughs, etc.) should be supplied to reduce wastage. Access to clean water is always essential and a source of calcium (ideally ground oyster shell) is highly recommended.

Control of Newcastle Disease (ND) and other health constraints.
Effective vaccines have been available against most strains of ND for a long time. However, there are a number of issues that need to be addressed:

1. Until recently, the potency of vaccines was highly sensitive to temperature which meant that the provision of an effective vaccine at village level required a 'cold chain' of refrigerators, cool boxes, etc., from the manufacturing laboratory through to the farm. The majority of vaccines are still highly sensitive to temperature and fall within this class.

2. Conventional vaccines are sold in large dose vials, usually 1 000 doses, aimed at the commercial producer but unsuitable for use at the village or household level.

3. Village flocks are usually small, scattered and multi-aged which makes them difficult to target by mass vaccination campaigns. Catching free range, often semi-feral chickens to vaccinate them individually has always proved difficult.

4. Vaccination of a multi-age flock has to be undertaken on a continuous basis (monthly) to be effective.

A new 'heat stable' oral vaccine has been developed and widely tested in Asia and Africa. The primary advantage is that it no longer requires a complete cold chain to maintain its potency. Queensland University in Australia has made available free to laboratories in developing countries a seed virus, designated I_2, to those who wish to explore the possibilities of vaccine production. This opens the door for producing with intermediate levels of technology, the fresh (not freeze-dried) vaccine at regional laboratories for use within a few weeks of production. In addition, a commercial V4 vaccine is also available, but not in large quantities and it remains expensive.

Potentially these vaccines offer the possibility of overcoming the problems of transport, storage and the difficulty of catching individual chickens. They are not, however, available everywhere, and applying the vaccine to feeds is not without problems. The question of who produces the vaccine remains an issue and experience has shown that projects may be able to introduce the technology but often production ceases once external inputs are removed.

Conventional vaccines remain a viable option if there is a reliable 'cold chain', if housing is provided that allows the birds to be caught easily and if sufficient numbers of owners participate, making the use of large vials economic. There is often little difference, however, in cost between 200- and 1 000-dose vials. A major problem with the larger vials is to find and catch 1 000 village chickens within the two hours or so that these 'old' heat sensitive vaccines remain viable.

Almost all birds in rural flocks are infected with a variety of internal parasites which cause reduced growth rate, weight loss and lower egg production. Strategically timed treatment(s) with inexpensive anthelmintics (e.g. fenbendazole and other benzimidazoles) given in the feed can easily eliminate the majority of these parasites.

Improved housing. The basic aim should be to provide simple (using local materials wherever possible) yet secure housing for the birds at night. Approximately $0.1m^2$ ($1ft^2$) should be adequate per bird. Housing should provide: perches for birds to roost on; access to clean water; a creep feed for chicks; and, nest boxes for laying and brooding. Location should be close to the house to deter theft and preferably raised off the ground to provide protection from predators and to reduce dampness. The shelter should have easy access to allow for catching the birds with the minimum of disturbance. Such housing can usually be provided cheaply using local materials (timber, mud, thatch, etc.); however, more complex designs may require more expensive sawn timber and wire netting.

Improved breeds. Once standard levels of husbandry (housing, feeding and disease control) have been achieved, improving the genetic potential of the birds offers the next step in increasing productivity. One strategy is to use local birds to incubate and rear higher egg-producing breeds.

Two choices are available. The introduction of pure-bred, dual-purpose breeds (e.g. the Rhode Island Red or Australorp) or the commercial hybrids, which are usually selected either for meat (broiler) or egg production. Traditionally, the dual-purpose breeds have been the exotic breeds of choice, the exception has been the White Leghorn, a laying breed that has proved unsatisfactory in adapting to village conditions. Obtaining grandparent stock of these breeds is becoming increasingly difficult and expensive. Some commercial companies now offer a more hardy, dual-purpose type of hybrid bird that could be used in certain situations.

Securing a regular source of healthy birds from well managed hatcheries can be problematic. Traditionally, government services have maintained poultry farms with imported parent stock and have supplied day-old-chicks (DOCs) or point-of-lay (POLs) birds to farmers. However, as with so many state run operations, there are real problems in managing such enterprises efficiently. Lack of working capital and staff incentives have resulted in most of them operating at a very low level of productivity and at a financial loss. The alternative of placing such activities in the private sector should be encouraged. Initially this may involve a phased approach through increasing cost-recovery to full privatization of government services. Non-governmental organizations can have a role in providing skills, start-up loans, etc., to assist private entrepreneurs in establishing themselves. Wherever possible the incubation, brooding, rearing and production of hatching eggs can be undertaken by separate specialized producers within the village.

In many developing countries improved birds have to be imported. There are a number of options that can be considered:

- *Importing grandparent stock to produce parent stock in the country.* This requires high levels of management, a regular supply of quality inputs, and a sufficient demand for parent stock.
- *Importing parent stock as either fertile eggs or day-old chicks to supply commercial birds for distribution.* This is usually the most economic option if acceptable levels of production can be maintained.
- *Importing commercial fertile eggs or day-old chicks for direct supply to farmers.* This option might be feasible in establishing a programme but it is costly. Although the full costs involved in producing DOCs locally from parent stock may exceed the cost of importing commercial DOCs if management and performance is low. With full cost recovery, these costs will have implications for the financial viability of the enterprise that must be understood.

There are other issues that also need to be considered. The indiscriminate distribution of imported breeds could have long-term adverse effects in diluting the advantageous traits in the indigenous breeds, especially broodiness in local hens.

There is potential for improving locally adapted breeds by selection. Virtually all the indigenous breeds have not been subjected to any selection process, other than natural selection. The consequence is that there is a large variation in production traits (i.e. number of eggs laid, etc.) between individuals in the overall population. By identifying and selecting the top performers for a given trait, and given the chicken's short generation interval, it would be possible to make substantial gains in genetic potential within the existing production environment. However, care must be taken since some traits are genetically negatively correlated i.e. broodiness and egg production. The logistical constraints in successfully implementing such a programme are formidable.

Institution support. The promotion and development of producer groups as the basis for self-sufficiency should be supported through training (technical and business management) and start-up capital in the form of goods or services. Involvement and support for the private sector in the provision of goods and services should be encouraged and, initially, this would involve the introduction of cost recovery for government goods and services that provide a 'private' rather than a 'public' benefit.

Chapter 2
Marketing quality eggs

QUALITY CRITERIA

Quality determines the acceptability of a product to potential customers. The quality of eggs and their stability during storage are largely determined by their physical structure and chemical composition. It is important therefore that those concerned with the handling of eggs are knowledgeable about this information in order to understand why eggs need to be treated in specific ways and to have a rational basis for day-to-day marketing decisions.

Composition and attributes of eggs

An egg consists of shell, membrane, albumen or white and yolk.

The shell. The shell of an egg has a rigid yet porous structure. The porous shell has great resistance to the entry of micro-organisms when kept dry and considerable resistance to the loss of moisture by evaporation. The colour of the shell, which may be white or brown depending on the breed of the laying chicken, does not affect quality, flavour, cooking characteristics, nutritional value or shell thickness.

Shell membrane. Inside the shell there are two membranes (as seen in Figure 6). The outer membrane is attached to the shell, the inner membrane is attached to the albumen or egg white. These two membranes provide a protective barrier against bacterial penetration.

Air space. An air space or air cell is a pocket of air usually found at the large end of the egg interior between the outer membrane and the inner membrane. This air cell is created by the contraction of the inner contents while the egg cools and by the evaporation of moisture after the egg has been laid. The air cell increases in size as time passes.

Figure 6
Egg composition

COMPOSITION

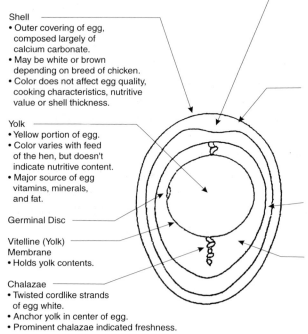

Shell
• Outer covering of egg, composed largely of calcium carbonate.
• May be white or brown depending on breed of chicken.
• Color does not affect egg quality, cooking characteristics, nutritive value or shell thickness.

Yolk
• Yellow portion of egg.
• Color varies with feed of the hen, but doesn't indicate nutritive content.
• Major source of egg vitamins, minerals, and fat.

Germinal Disc

Vitelline (Yolk) Membrane
• Holds yolk contents.

Chalazae
• Twisted cordlike strands of egg white.
• Anchor yolk in center of egg.
• Prominent chalazae indicated freshness.

Air Cell
• Pocket of air formed at the large end of egg.
• Caused by contraction of the contents during cooling after laying.
• Increases in size as egg ages.

Shell Membranes
• Two membranes – inner and outer shell membranes surround the albumen.
• Provide protective barrier against bacterial penetration.
• Air cell forms between these two membranes.

Thin Albumen (White)
• Nearest to the shell.
• Spreads around thick white of high-quality egg.

Thick Albumen (White)
• Major source of egg riboflavin and protein.
• Stands higher and spreads less in higher-grade eggs.
• Thins and becomes indistinguishable from thin white in lower-grade eggs.

Source: American Egg Board, www.aeg.org

Egg albumen or white. The albumen of the egg is composed of the outer thin albumen and the inner firm or thick albumen. The outer thin albumen spreads around the inner firm albumen. The inner firm albumen in high quality eggs stands higher and spreads less than the outer thin albumen.

White fibrous strips. These are twisted, cord-like strands of egg white, known as chalazae, which hold the yolk in position. Prominent thick chalazae indicate high quality and freshness.

Yolk. The yolk is almost spherical and is surrounded by a colourless membrane. The colour of the yolk varies with the type of feed given to the laying hen. If the laying hen is fed on maize, for example, the yolk will become a bright yellow. The colour of the yolk does not affect the nutritional content.

Egg weight. The weight of eggs varies widely depending on many factors such as the breed, the age of the layer and environmental temperature. In Africa, for example, the egg weight may range from 35 to 65 grams, while in Europe it may range from 45 to 70 grams. As a layer gets older the weight of the eggs increase as can be seen in the following figure.

Figure 7
Egg weight increase according to age of layer

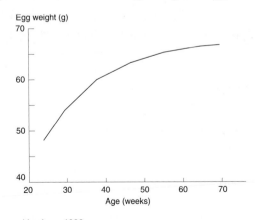

Source: Larbier and Leclecq, 1992

The components of an egg weighing 60 grams are made up as follows:

- yolk (29%) – 17.4 g
- white (61.5%) – 36.9 g
- shell (9.5%) – 5.6 g

Nutritional value

Eggs are a good source of high quality protein. They provide important sources of iron, vitamins and phosphorus. As a nutritional source of vitamin D, eggs rank second only to fish liver oils. Eggs are low in calcium, which is discarded in the shell, and contain very little vitamin C.

Eggs provide a unique and well-balanced source of nutrients for persons of all ages. Hard-cooked egg yolks are of great nutritional value as a major supplementary source of iron for infants. When children reach one year of age they may also be given egg whites. Eggs contain significant nutritional value, which is essential during rapid body growth, and therefore are excellent food for young children and teenagers.

Low caloric value, ease of digestibility and high nutrient content make eggs valuable in many therapeutic diets for adults. During convalescence, when bland diets may be required, eggs provide a good nutritious diet. For older people, whose caloric needs are lower, eggs are an easy, inexpensive and nutritious food to prepare and eat.

Availability, modest cost, ease of preparation, popular taste appeal and low caloric value give eggs a primary advantage for human nutritional needs.

Shell quality: texture, colour, shape and condition

The ideal shape of an egg as established by tradition and by practical considerations can be seen in Photograph 6.

Shell quality characteristics that must be considered are as follows:

- cleanliness
- soundness (unbroken)
- smoothness
- shape

The two most desirable shell qualities, cleanliness and soundness, are largely controlled by the production and handling of eggs. Eggs with shell defects should be removed from eggs destined to the retail trade. Clearly, consumers have adverse reactions to cracked or dirty eggs. Even if the cracks in an egg are only visible when candling, the micro-cracks may have serious consequences on quality. These eggs may be sold locally and possibly only a few hours after lay.

When the membrane is broken as well as the shell, the contents of the eggs can leak, and therefore the only practicable market outlet is sale as egg pulp. If the eggs are dirty, for example, with blood or faeces, consumers will react unfavourably to them.

Although shell colour is no indication of quality, consumers in some markets may prefer white eggs or brown eggs. In such circumstances, it is advisable to sort eggs by shell colour.

Yolk and albumen quality

In quality eggs the yolk should be round, firm and stand up well, and be yellow in colour.

There is often prejudice against very pale or deeply coloured yolks, however, there are some exceptions. In some Italian markets, for example, red yolks are a strong selling point. The yolk should have a pleasant, mild egg odour and flavour and should be surrounded by a large amount of upstanding thick white with only a small amount of thin white. The egg white should have the normal slightly green-yellow colour, though it may be slightly cloudy in appearance.

Consumers are generally very critical of any abnormal conditions in the egg yolk and white. Factors that may cause loss of quality are as follows:

- natural factors
- temperature
- humidity
- time
- handling
- storage
- tainting

Natural factors, for example, can be blood spots, which may range from small specks to a square centimetre in size. They may vary in colour from light grey to bright red and may be found in the yolk or in the egg white. "Blood eggs", with blood diffused throughout the white or spread around the yolk, are not commonly found and are generally rejected by the consumer. Photograph 7 shows the various degrees of spotting and blood diffusion.

Deterioration

The changes that occur in eggs stored for a week to ten days at a temperature between 27° and 29° C are comparable to those that occur in similar eggs in cold storage for several months at a temperature of − 1° C. The effect of temperature and storage on eggs can be seen in Photograph 8. The typical appearance of eggs stored up to 13 weeks at temperatures varying from 10° to 46° C can also be seen in this photograph. In advanced stages of deterioration, the thick white may disappear entirely and the yolk may enlarge to the point where its membranes are so weakened that it breaks when the egg is opened. Changes in odour and flavour take three or four weeks at a temperature of 21° C, or six to seven weeks at a temperature of 10° C to become noticeable to the ordinary consumer.

Temperature, humidity, air movement and storage time can all have adverse effects on interior quality. These factors, if not controlled, can cause loss of moisture in eggs. Loss of water through the porous shell will mean loss of weight. A loss of weight of two to three percent is common in marketing eggs and is hardly noticeable to consumers. However, enlarged air cells and a decreased size of egg contents become noticeable when losses exceed this extent.

Coating eggs with oil and other substances and storing them at low temperatures and high humidity may control moisture loss. The best conditions for storage are at a temperature of about − 1° C and relative humidity between 80 and 85 percent. At a temperature of 10° C, lower relative humidity is needed, between 75 and 80 percent. At all temperatures there is the risk of mould spoilage where the relative humidity is too high. Packaging materials that are too dry or are excessively moist and absorbent will also accentuate evaporation losses.

The contents of eggs when just laid are usually sterile and contain few organisms capable of causing spoilage even when the shells are slightly dirty or stained. The main cause of spoilage by bacteria is the washing of dirty eggs before marketing. When the egg is washed, organisms from water – usually bacteria – can penetrate the shell. Once inside they multiply and eventually spoil the egg, causing green, black and red rots. Even when eggs become wet without any cleaning process, for example, by condensation after removal from refrigerated storage into a warm temperature, conditions may be favourable for the penetration of micro-organisms and rotting may follow. When eggs are kept dry, no such way is provided for bacteria to penetrate the shell.

Mould spores normally present on eggshells may, if sufficient time elapses, germinate and grow, penetrating the shell and causing spoilage. Generally this occurs only when eggs are in cold storage for several months or more under conditions of high humidity (above 85 percent). It can occur, however, at any temperature if the humidity is sufficiently high and the holding time long enough.

Eggs can easily be tainted by strong odours from kerosene, gasoline, diesel oil, paint and varnish, and by such fruit and vegetables as apples, onions and potatoes. Special care must therefore be taken in storage, packaging materials and transport facilities used.

QUALITY MAINTENANCE

Maintaining fresh egg quality from producer to consumer is one of the major problems facing those engaged in marketing eggs. Proper attention to production, distribution and point-of-sale phases are of vital importance in maintaining egg quality.

Production factors

The factors that affect egg production are discussed in Chapter 1. The main production factors that affect quality maintenance are the following:

- breed
- age
- feed

- management
- disease control
- handling/collecting eggs
- housing

Breed. The breed of the laying hen affects shell colour; for example, Leghorns produce white eggs, while Rhode Island Reds produce brown eggs. The following egg quality factors are partly inherited: shell texture and thickness, the incidence of blood spots and the upstanding quality and relative amount of thick albumen. Though it may not always be possible, a consistent policy of selection for breeds by egg producers can bring noticeable improvements to quality.

Age. Birds typically begin producing eggs in their twentieth or twenty-first week and continue for slightly over a year. This is the best laying period and eggs tend to increase in size until the end of the egg production cycle. Birds lay fewer eggs as they near the moulting period. In the second year of lay, eggs tend to be of lower quality.

Feed. Egg quality and composition derive primarily from what a layer is fed. In terms of taste, for example, eggs laid by hens fed on fishmeal will have a "fishy" taste. The type of feed will also influence the shell of an egg and the colour of the yolk. Layers must be kept away from certain plant foods if egg colour defects are to be avoided. These may include cottonseed meal and the foliage of the *sterculiaceae* and *malvaceae* such as mallow weed.

Regular access to fresh or high-quality dehydrated green feed helps birds to produce eggs with a uniform yellow yolk. Yellow maize, alfalfa meal, and fresh grass provide good pigment sources for a normal yellowish-orange yolk colour.

Management. Good general management of the laying flock can improve egg quality. If birds are treated correctly and not put under conditions of stress they will produce properly.

Disease control. Diseases have an effect on egg quality. Infectious bronchitis and Newcastle disease, for example, will cause birds to lay eggs with poor quality shells and with extremely poor quality albumen. Many of the birds continue to lay poor quality eggs even after recovery. Effective vaccines should be administered.

Handling/collecting eggs. Frequent collection is essential each day in order to limit the number of dirty and damaged eggs and also to prevent the hens from eating the eggs. Careful handling is necessary in order to avoid breakage.

Laying house. The number of dirty eggs produced can be reduced significantly by providing good housing and clean nests for the layers. Cleaning and hygiene operations should be carried out frequently.

Measures to prevent deterioration during marketing

Temperature. By far the most effective method of minimizing deterioration of quality in eggs is to keep them at temperatures below 13° C. Eggs should never be left standing in the sun or in a room that gets very hot at some point in the day, but should be moved into shaded, well-ventilated rooms and underground cellars as quickly as possible. Various methods to prevent deterioration by temperature are shown below.

1. A simple method is covering eggs with green leaves, so as to reduce temperature.

2. A method commonly used is that of putting eggs in a porous pot where the outside of the pot is kept damp. Great care should be taken, however, to avoid the excess use of water, which could trickle down to the bottom of the pot damaging the eggs at the bottom.

3. Eggs can be kept in a wide-mouthed earthen pot that is buried in the ground up to half of its height. The inside of the pot is lined with a thin layer of grass to prevent the eggs being spoiled by excess moisture. Eggs are placed in the pot as soon as they are collected and the top covered with a thin

cloth to facilitate the exchange of air. A layer of sand and earth is spread around the earthen pot and water is sprinkled on it frequently during the day. The eggs are turned once a day to prevent the internal yolk of the egg from sticking to one side of the eggshell. Such a system may reduce the egg temperature by 8° C below the temperature outside the pot.

4. Another method that can be used which is ideal for dry climates makes use of the cooling effect of evaporation. Baskets of eggs are stored in a small wooden or wire-frame cupboard. A water tray is kept on top of the box and pieces of sacking are placed in the tray and arranged so that they hang on all sides of the box. More elaborate versions with arrangements for a steady dripping of water on to the sacking can be developed. This can be seen in Figure 8. In humid areas such devices would be less useful. The maintenance of egg quality in wet tropical areas is extremely difficult without refrigeration.

5. Refrigerated storerooms can be used if electricity is available. An example of a refrigerated storeroom is shown below. If refrigerated storehouses are not economically viable, the use of electric fans may be appropriate.

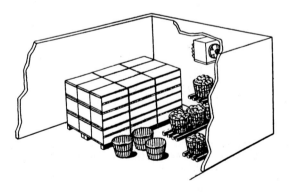

Refrigerated storeroom

Figure 8
Evaporation cooling in dry climates

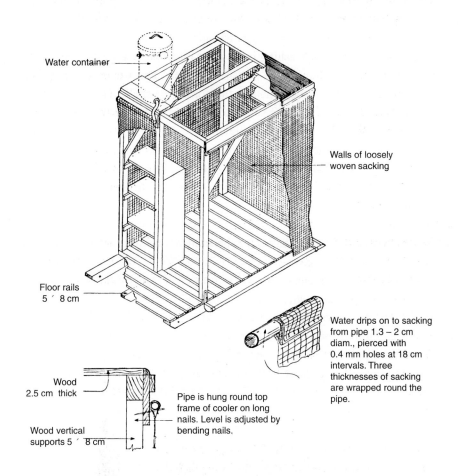

Water container

Walls of loosely
woven sacking

Floor rails
5 ´ 8 cm

Water drips on to sacking
from pipe 1.3 – 2 cm
diam., pierced with
0.4 mm holes at 18 cm
intervals. Three
thicknesses of sacking
are wrapped round the
pipe.

Wood
2.5 cm thick

Pipe is hung round top
frame of cooler on long
nails. Level is adjusted by
bending nails.

Wood vertical
supports 5 ´ 8 cm

The cooler should be shaded from direct sunlight. It is most efficient when air circulates *freely* round it and does not give good results in a closed room. The cooling effect can be intensified by blowing air through damp sacking with an electric fan.

Producers, wholesalers and retailers should move eggs to consumers as quickly as possible to minimize the risk of spoilage. The importance of avoiding delays at all stages in the distribution channel cannot be overemphasized and should be the primary consideration determining marketing arrangements.

Treatment of dirty eggs. Some eggs will inevitably have dirty shells. For the purpose of appearance, washing is the most effective and simplest method of removing dirt and stains from the shell surface. The water, however, may contain bacteria that could penetrate the porous eggshell causing it to decay. Odourless detergent-sanitizing substances should be used in the water to wash eggs, but these may be difficult to obtain.

Eggs can be submerged in clean hot water (water temperature should be around 38° C); however, this may cause thermal cracks in the eggshell and internal expansion of the egg content. It is better to avoid washing eggs altogether. Using dry abrasives for scraping and brushing may be the optimal solution. In using this method, care should be taken to avoid removing excessive shell material, which will weaken the shell and increase the rate of evaporation.

Shell oiling. Coating eggs with a thin film of oil greatly reduces losses by evaporation, especially where eggs are in cold storage for several months or are held at temperatures above 21° C. Special odourless, colourless, low-viscosity mineral oils should be used. Where eggs must withstand high temperatures, they should be oiled from four to six hours after lay. If eggs are to be stored at a temperature of 0° C, they should be oiled 18 to 24 hours after lay. Eggs can be oiled by hand dipping wire baskets or by machine. The temperature of the oil should be at least 11° C above that of the eggs. Before the oil is reused it should be heated to a temperature of 116° C to prevent bacteria survival and then be filtered. The oil reservoirs should be cleaned properly. In terms of appearance oiled eggs differ from other eggs only in the slight shine left on the eggshells by the more viscous oils.

Inducements for quality maintenance

Provision of effective incentives for the adoption of quality maintenance procedures is the function of the marketing system. It must provide some means whereby egg quality can be appraised and a system of purchasing premiums and deductions applied accordingly. Methods of assessing quality of eggs are discussed below.

GRADING AND STANDARDIZATION

Grading and standardization consist of arranging produce into a number of uniform categories according to physical and quality characteristics of economic importance. It is a process of identification, classification and separation.

The advantages of grading and standardization are as follows.

- Different grade eggs may be sold to different customers. Customers willing to pay more for high quality eggs will be served. On the other hand, eggs with micro-cracks or small blood spots may be sold to bakeries.
- Setting and maintaining a reliable standard creates consumer confidence in the product and a favourable reputation. This will enable buyers (wholesalers, retailers, exporters, consumers) to purchase a reliable product that they recognize and may well avoid inspection and disputes.
- The ability to furnish an accurate description of eggs in storage may help in obtaining credit.

Grade specifications

The value factors most generally appreciated in eggs are internal quality, appearance and soundness of shell, size and colour.

Most egg marketing systems find it advantageous to adopt grading practices that:

- eliminate inedible and defective eggs;
- separate eggs into high and lower acceptable categories; and
- establish uniform weight classifications.

For example, the grading system used in the United States of America, as recommended by the United States Department of Agriculture (USDA), is summarized in Table 7.

Table 7
Summary of United States grade standards for individual shell eggs

Specifications for each quality factor			
Quality Factor	**AA Quality**	**A Quality**	**B Quality**
Shell	Clean.	Clean.	Clean to slightly stained.*
	Unbroken.	Unbroken.	Unbroken.
	Practically normal.	Practically normal.	Abnormal.
Air Cell	1/8 inch or less in depth.	3/16 inch or less in depth.	over 3/16 inch in depth.
	Unlimited movement and free or bubbly.	Unlimited movement and free or bubbly.	Unlimited movement and free or bubbly.
White	Clear.	Clear.	Weak and watery.
	Firm.	Reasonably firm.	Small blood and meat spots present.**
Yolk	Outline slightly defined.	Outline fairly well defined.	Outline plainly visible.
	Practically free from defects.	Practically free from defects.	Enlarged and flattened.
			Clearly visible germ development but not blood.
			Other serious defects.

For eggs with dirty or broken shells, the standards of quality provide two additional qualities.

Dirty	Check
Unbroken. Adhering dirt or foreign material, prominent stains, moderately stained areas in excess of B quality.	Broken or cracked shell, but membranes intact, not leaking.***

* Moderately stained areas permitted (1/32 of surface if localized, or 1/16 if scattered).
** If they are small (aggregating not more than 1/8 inch in diameter).
*** Leaker has broken or cracked shell membranes, and contents leaking or free to leak.

Note: Measurements in inches: 1/8 inch = 3 mm, 3/16 inch = 6 mm.
Source: United States Department of Agriculture

The various egg sizes according to weight used in the United States are as follows:

- Jumbo = 70 g and above
- Extra large = 65-70 g
- Large = 56-65 g
- Medium = 49-56 g
- Small = 42-49 g
- Peewee = 35-42 g

Of course different size specifications and quality factors vary from country to country; for example, the various sizes according to weight used in Africa are as follows:

- Large = 65 g and above
- Medium = 55-65 g
- Small = 45-55 g

Quality specifications development

A simple set of quality specifications might be set up as follows.

First Grade. The shell must be clean, unbroken and practically normal in shape and texture. The air cell must not exceed 9.5 mm in depth and may move freely, but not be broken and bubbly. The yolk may appear off-centre, but only slightly enlarged, and may show only slight embryonic development. No foreign objects may be present.

Second Grade. The shell must be unbroken, but may be somewhat abnormal in shape and texture. Only slight stains and marks are permitted. The yolk may appear dark and enlarged and may show embryonic development, but not at the blood vessel stage and beyond. Blood spots less then 6mm in diameter are permitted.

Third grade. Other edible eggs are permitted, that is, those that are not rotted, mouldy or musty. Also, those eggs that are not incubated to blood vessel stage, and those not containing insects, worms or blood spots 6mm in diameter, are permitted.

Interior quality

The most accurate test of interior quality is the break-out method – open the egg on to a flat glass surface and compare the appearance of the yolk and white with that shown for various quality levels as shown in Figure 9.

A more simple side-view comparison of egg quality can be seen in Figure 10.

In marketing, however, the above method can only be used on a sample basis. A method that does not require egg breaking is more appropriate.

Candling

Candling is the only method of testing eggs for quality, internally and externally, without breaking them. It consists of inspecting an egg with a beam of light that makes the interior quality visible. A very simple form of candling is placing a candle in a dark room and positioning an egg in front of the flame and looking at the interior quality. A simple candling device can be seen below.

Candling box

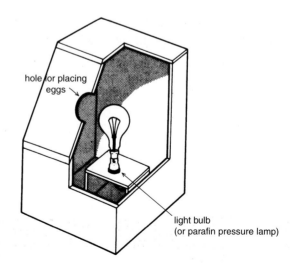

hole for placing eggs

light bulb
(or parafin pressure lamp)

Source: Kekeocha, 1985

Figure 9
Interior quality of eggs by United States standards

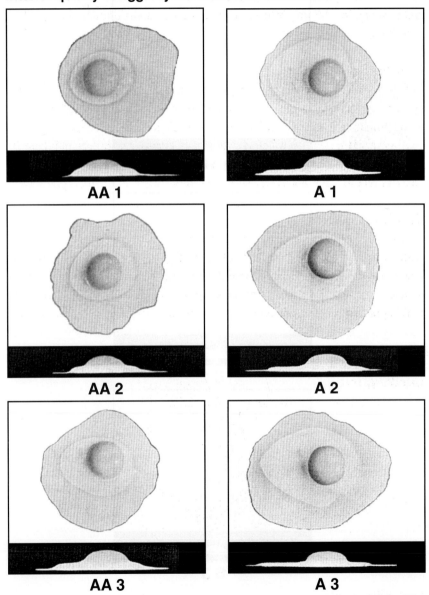

Figure 9, continued

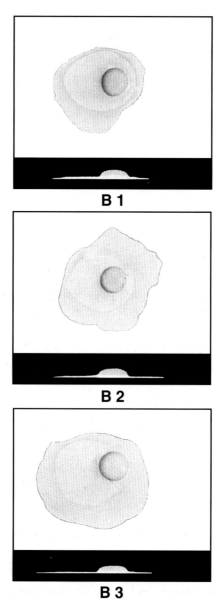

B 1

B 2

B 3

Source: USDA

Figure 10
Side view for egg quality

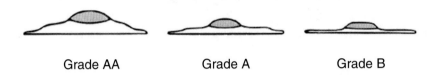

Grade AA   Grade A   Grade B

Source: American Egg Board, www. aeb.org

If electricity is available, a light bulb can be placed in the box, otherwise a paraffin lamp or candle can be enclosed in a casing. The hole in the box should be about 3 cm in diameter, sufficient for egg sizes ranging from 40 to 70 grams. The light will shine out of the hole making the interior egg quality visible.

Candling method. Pick four eggs to be candled and put two in each hand. Place the first egg near the candling box hole with the large end of the egg held against the light, and with the axis at a 45° angle so that the egg has light shining through it. Twirl the egg so as to observe defects which otherwise might not be observed. If first egg candled is free of defects, roll the first egg back in to the palm of the hand. Meanwhile, the second egg in the other hand should be brought to the light and examined. While the second egg is up against the light, the third egg in the other hand should be brought into candling position. Photograph 9 shows how to hold eggs while candling.

Although the beginner will soon learn to detect such things as cracked shells and bloodspots, considerable training is needed before internal quality can be estimated with reasonable accuracy. Photograph 10 shows the appearance of eggs of various quality in candling.

The main interior quality points to be observed in candling can be summarized as follows:

Yolk. The judgement of internal quality is based mainly on the visibility, ease of movement and shape of yolk. Common yolk faults are the following:

- *Sided* – displaced to an appreciable extent from its normal central position.
- *Stuck* – on twirling the egg, it may be found that the yolk is stuck to the inner shell membrane.
- *Patchy* – uneven in colour, including defects sometimes described as "heat spots."
- *Abnormal in shape* – flattened or irregular and in extreme cases may be broken and dispersed in the white.
- *Discoloured* – of a dark or greyish appearance often with a very distinct outline.
- *Embryonic development* – first shows as a dark halo round the germ cell near the centre of the yolk and later as thin blood vessels and a bright blood ring.

White. In practice, the quality of egg white is judged by the degree of movement of the yolk and by the definition of its outline. Common faults in egg white are as follows:

- *Discoloured* – definitely tinted grey, yellow, green or brown.
- *Cloudy* – muddy or streaky. Usually this condition indicates potential rot, but washing an egg in very hot water can cause a similar appearance.

Air cell. The depth of the air cell is a rough indication of the age of the egg and there is often a relation between this depth and the internal quality. Hence, the depth of the air cell is taken into account in candling, but other indications of quality are given equal weight. The air cell may be:

- *Large* – exceeding 6 mm in depth.
- *Running* – if the air cell is broken, one or more air bubbles will be found in the white. If the air cell has forced its way between the two shell membranes, bubbles will move around the shell when the egg is candled.

A running air cell, however, may be caused by rough handling and should not exclude the egg from a high-grade class.

- *Ringed* – the air cell is very large, sharply defined and with grey or brown edges.

Other common defects of internal quality that may be found are listed here:

- *Blood spots* – clots or streaks of blood in the white or adhering to the yolk.
- *Blood egg* – blood is diffused throughout the white or spread around the yolk.
- *Meat spots* – fatty material, fleshy or liver-like that may be found floating freely in the white, embedded in the chalazae or attached to the yolk.
- *Staleness* – in most cases the air cell is abnormally large, clearly defined and often ringed. As a rule the yolk is sided and its outline clearly defined.
- *Mould growth* – usually grey or black in colour, but can occasionally be pinkish, found on the outside and inside of the shell or shell membranes.
- *Rot* – usually violet, green, red or blue in colour. The early stages of a rot are less easy to detect, but any egg with a streaky, turbid white should be rejected. The egg may have an unpleasant smell even if unbroken.
- *Taint* – the egg has an abnormal odour.

Photographs 11 through 14 show examples of various egg quality deficiencies that can be seen when candling.

Shell condition. Weak, rough, mouldy, cracked and deformed shells may be detected as eggs are picked up for candling. But with candling small or micro-cracks on the eggshell can be seen. A typical deformed eggshell can be seen in Photograph 15.

Another method of verifying shell soundness is that of gently hitting two eggs together (belling). A dull sound instead of clear clinking indicates a cracked egg.

Developing a standardized system

Any system used to grade the quality and weight of eggs is only effective if it ensures that consumers obtain eggs of the quality and kind they want. This requires that three conditions be met.

1. The initial classification must be correct.
2. There should be no appreciable deterioration between time of grading and time of sale.
3. The consumers should have a clear guide to the quality of produce they are purchasing.

In developing a grading system, the following preparations are vital.

- Study thoroughly the pattern of production, consumption and trade.
- Work out grade specifications in close consultation with those traders who would be likely to take advantage of them.
- Qualified inspectors are needed to ensure that conformity with the grades indicated is upheld. Producers and packers who accept their inspection can be authorized to apply approved grade stamps.
- Legislation should be enacted to prevent the possibility of misleading labelling. Certain standards may be made obligatory, for example, minimum standards to protect consumers from unwholesome and dangerous foods.
- Finally, if consumers are to take full advantage of a grading system, the grade indications should be clear and easily understood.

It is important that eggs are not allowed to deteriorate below the grade indicated before they reach the consumer. Under conditions of high humidity with temperatures of 32° C and above, eggs being distributed may undergo considerable deterioration in only a few days. Under such circumstances, the inspection of eggs held for more than three or four days must be clearly and responsibly assigned.

Equipment and candling layout

In order to grade and pack eggs with consistent accuracy, speed and economy, it is essential that adequate facilities be provided. These include a semi-darkened room, without stray illumination, that is well equipped with bench and shelf space and with good facilities for handling of eggs and recording results. The candling device, if possible, should be adjustable and mounted at such a height that the beam of light when emerging horizontally from the device arrives at about the height of the operator's elbow. The lamp or light bulb in the candling box should be kept clean. An operator should use the same candling apparatus every day to help minimize errors. Each operator must have enough room to move freely and handle packing materials and boxes. Efficiency can be increased by installing partitions between candling benches, arranging supplies of packing materials conveniently and by providing for the easy disposal of damaged materials. Floors and walls should have smooth, hard non-reflecting surfaces and be rounded at intersections. Thorough cleanliness is essential to prevent bad odours. Good ventilation should be provided.

The candling bench should be designed to particular needs. Where there are only a few candling benches, operators themselves can obtain eggs and supplies from nearby stocks and carry away completed egg cases. As the volume handled increases, however, it usually becomes more efficient to assign a special worker to service the candlers.

Chapter 3
Egg packaging, transport and storage

PACKAGING OF SHELL EGGS

Nature has given the egg a natural package – the shell. Despite its relative strength, the egg is an extremely fragile product and even with the best handling methods, serious losses can result from shell damage. Economical marketing generally requires that eggs be protected by the adoption of specialized packaging and handling procedures.

Functions of packaging

Packaging is an important component in delivering quality eggs to buyers. It embraces both the art and science of preparing products for storage, transport and eventually sale. Packaging protects the eggs from:

- micro-organisms, such as bacteria;
- natural predators;
- loss of moisture;
- tainting;
- temperatures that cause deterioration; and
- possible crushing while being handled, stored or transported.

Proper handling and storage, as seen in the previous chapter, help control moisture loss, but appropriate packaging may also help prevent it. Eggs also need to breathe, hence the packaging material used must allow for the entrance of oxygen. The material used must be clean and odourless so as to prevent possible contamination and tainting. Authentic egg packaging materials can be reused, but careful attention must be paid to possible damage, odours and cleanliness. The packaging must be made to withstand handling, storage and transport methods of the most diverse kind and to protect the eggs against temperatures that cause deterioration and humidity. Finally, consumers like to see what they are buying, especially if it concerns fresh produce. An egg package should be designed so that the customers not only recognize the product as such, but can also see the eggs they are buying.

Many factors must be taken into consideration for packaging eggs. It is important to obtain information regarding the necessary requirements for a particular market, such as:

- quality maintenance;
- storage facilities;
- type of transport;
- distance to be travelled;
- climatic conditions;
- time involved; and
- costs.

Egg packages

There are many different types of egg packages, which vary both in design and packaging material used.

Type 1. Packing eggs with clean and odourless rice husks, wheat chaff or chopped straw in a firm walled basket or crate greatly decreases the risk of shell damage. An example of this can be seen in the forefront of Photograph 16.

It is also be possible to pack eggs in a simple basket as seen in Photograph 17. The basket has no cushioning material such as straw and therefore damage to the eggs may occur more easily. This kind of packaging may be fit for short distance transport.

Type 2. A very common form of packaging is the filler tray. The fillers are then placed in boxes or cases. An example can be seen in Photograph 18.

Filler trays are made of wood pulp moulded to accommodate the eggs. They are constructed so that they can be stacked one on top of the other and can also be placed in boxes ready for transport. Filler trays also offer a convenient method for counting the eggs in each box, without having to count every single egg. Usually the standard egg tray carries 36 eggs. Therefore, if a box holds five trays, for example, the box has a total of 180 eggs (36 x 5 = 180).

The cases used may be made of sawn wood; however, they are more commonly made of cardboard. When using cardboard cases, special care must be taken in stacking so that excessive weight is not placed on a case at the bottom of a stack.

Fillers can also be made of plastic as seen in Photograph 19. The advantages of using plastic egg fillers are that they can be reused and are washable. The fillers can be covered with plastic coverings and be used as packages for final sale to the buyer. More importantly, however, plastic transparent fillers allow for the inspection of eggs without handling or touching the eggs.

Type 3. Eggs can also be packed in packages that are smaller and specific for retail sale. Each package can hold from two to twelve eggs. These cases can be made of paperboard or moulded wood pulp as seen in Photograph 20, or can be made of plastic as shown in Photograph 21.

It is also possible to pack eggs in small paperboard cases and cover them with plastic film. Egg cases have also been developed from polystyrene. The advantages of using polystyrene are superior cushioning and protection against odours and moisture. The package is also resistant to fungus and mould growth.

The use of small cases is restricted by availability and cost considerations. However, small cases are good for retailers and customers. They are easy for the retailers to handle and customers are able to inspect the eggs.

Labelling

Labels are a source of important information for the wholesaler, retailer and consumer and not just pieces of paper stuck onto cartons or boxes. The important facts on the label contain information for buyers concerning the eggs, their size and weight and quality/grade description – AA, A or B. Labels may also indicate the producer, when the eggs were laid, how to store them and their expiration date. Persuading the buyer to purchase the product without tasting, smelling or touching is another function of labelling.

A sample label can be seen here below:

Africa Eggs
6 Fresh Brown Eggs
Size: Medium
AA Class Eggs
Net weight 300 g
Produced by Af. Ric.a. Eggs
Nairobi, Kenya.

Labels can be either printed directly on cartons or attached to the cartons. The cost of labelling must be taken into consideration. Simple methods of labelling are available such as stencil or stamp as can be seen below.

Stencil and stamp labelling

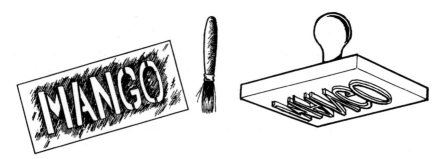

Source: Fellows and Axel, 1993

Costs of packaging

When calculating the costs of packaging, expenses must be considered for:

- packaging materials;
- labelling;
- labour;
- additional working capital required;
- changing existing facilities (if applicable); and
- packaging machinery (if applicable).

STORAGE OF EGGS

The storage of shell eggs during the main laying season, in order to conserve them for consumption when they are scarce, has been practised for many centuries.

For the successful storage of eggs, the following conditions must be met.

- The eggs placed in storage must be clean; they must not be washed or wet.
- Packaging material used should be new, clean and odourless.
- Loss of water due to evaporation should be reduced to a minimum.
- The storage room must be free from tainting products and materials and should be cleaned regularly with odourless detergent sanitizers.
- The storage room must be kept at a constant temperature and humidity must be checked.
- There should be air circulation in the storage room.
- Eggs should be stored so that they are allowed to breathe.
- As far as possible, interior quality should be monitored; there should be a good proportion of thick white, the yolk should stand up well, and the flavour of white and yolk should be good.

If all of the above requirements are to be met, refrigerated storage is necessary.

Cold storage of eggs

In the tropics, eggs can deteriorate very quickly unless they are stored at low temperatures. The ideal temperature for storage in such climates is 13°C or lower (usually between 10° and 13° C). Here refrigeration is a necessity for successful commercial storage; however, it may be unavailable or the costs too high.

The most important factors in successful cold storage are as follows.

- The selection and packaging of eggs.
- The equipment and preparation of the cold store.
- Proper temperature, humidity and air circulation.
- Periodic testing for quality.
- The gradual adjustment of eggs to higher temperatures when removed from storage.

The selection and packaging of eggs for storage. Eggs for storage must be clean, of good interior quality and have a sound shell. If they are to be stored for more then a month, they should be equivalent to the U.S. grade A (see Chapter 2, Table 7). Therefore, it is best to candle all eggs before storage. It may also be advisable to take a sample and to break out these eggs as a further quality check (see Chapter 2). The period of time between laying and storage should not be more than a few days. The eggs should be kept cool during that time.

Packaging materials used for storage should be new, clean, odourless and free from damage. When packaging material is reused, it is extremely important that it is clean, odourless and free from damage. It is important that the material used allow the eggs to "breathe" and to be free from tainting odours. It should also be sturdy in the event that the cases have to be stockpiled on top of one another.

The equipment and preparation of the cold store. The storage room should have a concrete floor that is washable. Walls and ceilings must also be washable. Wooden buildings have been found to be satisfactory, provided they do not impart foreign odours or flavours to the eggs. The room should be scrubbed thoroughly with hot water and soap or an odourless detergent sanitizer before being used. A final rinse with a hypochlorite solution will help greatly in deodorizing the storeroom. A liberal application of freshly slaked lime to unpainted plaster surfaces will also help. The storage room should be aired and dried out thoroughly after cleaning, then closed up and the refrigeration turned on. It is best to allow several days for the temperature and humidity to stabilize before introducing the eggs.

Proper temperature, humidity and air circulation. Careful and accurate control of the air condition is essential. A temperature between $-1.5°$ and $-0°$ C is recommended. At a temperature of $-2.5°$ C eggs freeze. The room should be well constructed and insulated and the refrigeration should be capable of maintaining an adequate uniform temperature in all areas. The cases of eggs should be separated by wood-strips and kept well away from the walls so as not to obstruct air circulation. Aisles left for the convenience of handling specific egg cases also help air circulation. Periodic ventilation of the storage room is advisable to promote air exchange.

The relative humidity should be between 80 and 85 percent at a cold storage temperature of $-1°$ C. At cold storage temperatures of about $10°$ C the relative humidity should be between 75 and 80 percent. In such instances, on average, egg weight loss should not exceed 0.5 percent per month. During the early stages of storage when the packaging material is absorbing moisture at a high rate, the floors should be sprinkled with clean water several times a day. If forced-air circulation is feasible, a controlled temperature water-spray air washer may be used. If the humidity becomes excessive, part of the air can be cycled through a unit containing calcium chloride. Where eggs have been oiled less attention can be paid to the humidity level.

Periodic testing for quality. Periodic quality checks are essential if the risk of heavy egg losses is to be avoided. Every month or so a sample of eggs should be selected from the various lots and tested. Usually a sample of about 1 percent of all eggs in storage may be sufficient. For example, if 3 000 eggs are kept in storage, 30 eggs sampled from various egg cases will enable a good estimation of the general quality level of the eggs. If there is evidence of excessive deterioration, it is best to dispose of the eggs quickly, after eliminating those that are unfit for consumption.

The gradual adjustment of eggs to higher temperatures. Care must be taken in removing eggs from storage to avoid the condensation of moisture on shells. This is minimized by raising the temperature slowly or by moving the eggs through rooms with intermediate temperatures. If condensation occurs, the eggs should be held under conditions that allow the moisture to evaporate within a day or so.

As indicated earlier, eggs should not be stored with products that may taint them. For the long term, eggs are best stored alone, while for the short term they may be kept with dairy products such as milk and mild-flavoured cheese. The average storage life for eggs is between six and seven months.

Economics of cold storage

There is a tendency to underestimate the difficulties involved in providing good cold storage facilities and to recommend their installation without adequate investigation of their cost and potential economic return. The following factors should be considered when contemplating cold storage.

- Refrigeration is a complex and highly technical business.
- Capital investment and operating costs must be estimated.
- Potential available business must be appraised.

The potential available business must be appraised as well as its distribution over the different seasons of the year and the costs involved. Egg storage to even out the availability of supplies is likely to provide business for only a part of the year. The average – not maximum – price difference between the plentiful and scarce seasons must be calculated. If projected returns do not significantly exceed the costs envisaged for storage, there is little incentive for egg traders to make use of storage.

It must be considered that some egg producers, according to their circumstances and possibilities, maintain yearly production through special breeding and feeding programmes and by providing illumination in the hen laying houses. This may even out the rate of egg production throughout the year and hence long-term storage should not be considered.

Layout of packaging and storing facilities for shell eggs

A model layout of a packaging and storing room for shell eggs is seen below.

Figure 11
Layout of packaging and storage facility

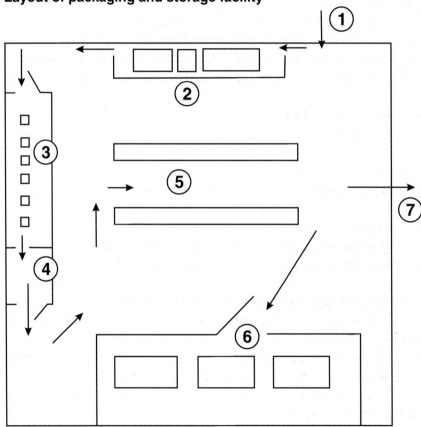

1. Eggs enter the packing/storage facility
2. Temporary store room
3. Candling room
4. Weighing/cleaning room
5. Packaging area
6. Long-term storage
7. Eggs ready for transport

The layout for the packaging and storing facility is of great importance for efficient and effective management. The various rooms should be kept clean, well ventilated and, where necessary, refrigeration provided. All personnel working in the facility should wear clean outer garments, use caps or head bands and wash their hands when handling eggs and equipment. All equipment used should be clean.

1. ***Eggs enter the packing/storage room.*** Eggs from production are brought into the packing/storage facility. Eggs can be brought in by hand or by conveyor belt. In intensive egg production, the birds lay eggs that roll out of the cage onto conveyor belts, which transport the eggs directly to the packing/storage facilities. This can be seen in Photograph 22. Photograph 23 shows how eggs could be stacked for manual movement if brought in by hand from production to the packing/storage facilities.

2. ***Temporary storage room.*** Here eggs are stored temporarily before they are moved to the candling room.

3. ***Candling room.*** Eggs are brought into the candling room, where candlers verify the interior and external quality of eggs. The small squares (see Figure 11, No. 3) represent candling benches. The candling machine in Photograph 24 is used in fully mechanized or semi-mechanized systems, where the eggs are brought onto the candling machine by a conveyor belt.

4. ***Cleaning/weighing room.*** After candling, eggs are transported by conveyor belts to the cleaning/weighing room. Here eggs are cleaned with abrasives, where possible, and sorted by weight. Usually the size indicates which category eggs should fall into – small, medium or large. This can be done by hand; however, automated weighing machinery is available.

5. ***Packaging area.*** After weighing, the eggs are taken to the packaging area. Packaging can be done either by hand (see Photograph 25) or automatically by machinery. As seen in Photograph 26 the eggs arrive at machine No. 1. If we look at Photograph 27, there are three weighing machines numbered

one to three. Each machine is set to pack only predetermined egg weights. For example, machine No.1 (see Photograph 26) packs only 60-gram eggs. If the eggs are below that weight, they will be conveyed to machine No. 2 (see Photograph 28). The eggs are then packed automatically.

After packing, eggs may either be kept in long-term storage (No. 6 in Figure 11) or may be ready for immediate transport (No.7 in Figure 11).

TRANSPORT OF EGGS

For the successful transport of shell eggs three essential requirements must be met.

1. The containers and packaging materials must be such that the eggs are well protected against mechanical damage.

2. Care should be taken at all stages of handling and transport. Workers handling eggs should be instructed so that they appreciate the need for careful handling. The provision of convenient loading platforms at packing stations, loading depots and railing stations, and handling aids, such as hand trucks and lifts, are of great help.

3. The eggs must be protected at all times against exposure to temperatures that cause deterioration in quality as well as contamination, especially tainting.

The permissible range of temperatures during loading and transport depends on the local climatic conditions and the duration of the journey. Table 8 shows recommended temperatures for transport and loading.

Care is needed to avoid excessive shaking, especially where roads are bad. Egg containers should be stacked tightly and tied down securely to minimize movement. Covers should be used to protect them from the heat of the sun, rain and extreme cold where applicable. Where bicycles are used, a device such as a special carrier suspended on springs may be helpful.

Table 8
Recommended temperatures for loading and transport

	Transport over 2 or 3 days	Transport over 5 or 6 days
Maximum on loading	+6° C	+3° C
Recommended for transport	-1° to + 3° C	-1° to + 1° C
Acceptable for transport	1° to + 6° C	1° to + 3° C

A basic prerequisite for all long-distance transport is that arrangements be made for proper reception, handling and storage at the end of the journey. This is especially important where large lots are delivered to a relatively small market. Without access to suitable storage facilities, the eggs may have to be marketed quickly under adverse climatic conditions, which may cause substantial quality deterioration and price losses.

Delivery of high quality eggs over long distances, especially in hot climates, generally calls for refrigeration. Requirements for the successful operation of refrigerated transport equipment are rather rigid especially as regards the following factors:

- efficiency and durability of insulation;
- adequacy and reliability of the cooling mechanism; and
- adequate circulation of air within the vehicle or container so that variations of temperature are slight.

Decisions on the establishment of new refrigerated transport services for eggs should be based on thorough economic as well as technical evaluations.

The following criteria should be taken into consideration.

- The need for a managerial and operational staff that is competent in all the operations involved in assembling, loading and distributing.
- The necessity of a sufficient volume of trade throughout the year.
- The possibility of making up loads with other compatible produce, e.g. dairy products.
- The possibility of carrying return loads, once eggs have been distributed.
- The degree to which the demand for refrigerated transport is concentrated geographically.

Chapter 4
Marketing organization for eggs

The greater the distance between producer and consumer, the more complex is the marketing organization required to ensure that eggs reach consumers in the form, place and time desired. Producers may decide to market their produce directly to consumers – direct marketing – or may choose from a variety of marketing organizations that make up a marketing channel.

Direct marketing includes the following methods of selling:

- sales from the farm (farm gate);
- door-to-door sales;
- producers' markets; and
- sales to local retail shops.

A typical marketing channel is made up of:

- collectors;
- assembly merchants;
- wholesalers; and
- retailers.

Figure 12
Direct marketing

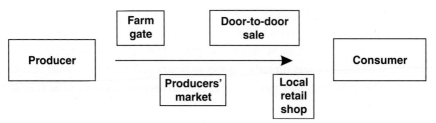

Figure 13
Organized marketing channel

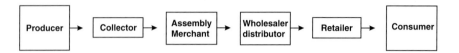

DIRECT MARKETING

Egg producers who are situated a short distance from consumers may be able to practise direct marketing. Before choosing to sell their products directly to consumers, however, they must evaluate two main factors:

- *Time.* Producers who choose direct marketing have less time for production activities.
- *Cost.* The costs involved in direct marketing.

There are four main ways to carry out direct marketing.

Sales from the farm

Producers may be able to sell eggs directly from the farm (farm gate). This, however, will depend on whether consumers are able and willing to go to the producer's facilities. The main advantage of farm-gate selling is that the producer may be able to obtain a market price for eggs without incurring marketing costs. The main advantage for the consumers is that eggs will be fresh with little or no quality loss.

Door-to-door sales/street hawking

Some consumers prefer that eggs be brought directly to their door. This means that the producer must spend time on marketing; however, consumers may appreciate the service and be willing to pay a good price. Furthermore, the producer can take orders directly from consumers and carry only what he/she is assured will be bought. Eggs may also be sold on the street as can be seen in Photograph 30.

Producers' markets

Usually the producer simply occupies a stall in a public marketplace and offers his/her produce for sale. Eggs are commonly displayed in baskets and often differentiated by weight/size and colour (see Photograph 31). Sales in producers' markets permit a farmer to make direct contact with consumers who are not able to go to the production facilities. The main disadvantage of using such markets is that, towards the end of the day, the producer may have to either reduce his prices sharply to dispose of remaining stock or carry it back to the farm.

Sales to local retail shops

Producers can also sell directly to local retail shops. This requires some sort of agreement between the two parties regarding constant supply, quality and payment methods.

In some cases it may be possible for producers to sell directly to institutional consumers such as hotels, restaurants, schools and hospitals. This type of direct marketing, however, requires negotiation, which may result in a written contract of the duties and obligations of both parties. It also requires continual interaction over time between producer and buyer, a standard egg quality agreement and a constant supply. The producer must carefully evaluate the issues involved including the regular production and transport of large quantities of eggs.

MARKETING CHANNELS

A marketing channel is composed of a set of separate but interdependent organizations involved in the process of making a product available to consumers. The use of a marketing channel is convenient particularly when the producer does not have the time or financial means to carry out direct marketing. Intermediaries are usually able to make the product widely available and accessible because they are specialized and have experience and contacts. They also have a better understanding of the egg market. Intermediaries take the risks involved in marketing and also pay for the produce immediately.

MARKETING INTERMEDIARIES
Collectors

Collectors undertake the initial work of assembling eggs from various producers or local country markets. They operate either on a commission basis or by purchasing on their own account. Where the quantity of eggs collected at each stop is small and frequent, this system is often the most economic. Collectors may be itinerant merchants, producers themselves, assembly merchants, wholesalers or their agents, or retailers.

Assembly merchants

Assembly merchants may be divided into the following categories: local assembly market; independent processor-packer; and, cooperative processor-packer.

Local assembly market. In a typical local assembly market, a private firm, a producers' cooperative or a municipality provides an enclosed space for the use of sellers. Sales may take place by public auction or by private negotiation, subject to rules such as those on quality and payment arrangements. Auctioning requires the eggs to be graded and possibly presented in standardized containers, marked with identifying names or symbols. The local assembly market may provide cold storage facilities for the convenience of market users.

Independent processor-packer. This type of enterprise usually purchases eggs either through collectors or directly from producers. The processor-packer may pass by the farm and pick up the eggs or the producer may deliver the eggs to the processing facilities where they are graded and packed. Usually eggs are sold to wholesalers; however, they are also sold directly to retailers and institutional consumers such as hotels, restaurants and hospitals.

Cooperative processor-packer. The same type of enterprise may be set up and run by a cooperative association of producers. The main advantage is that the business is run by and for those who use it, rather than by those who own it. Cooperatives can obtain financing, provide extra competition to independent processor-packers and provide an alternative to established intermediaries.

Before forming a cooperative, producers should carefully evaluate:

- the market for eggs;
- problems in existing marketing channels and how to remedy them;
- the degree of know-how that producers have in marketing;
- rules and regulations;
- legal status;
- availability of finances;
- staffing requirements; and
- appropriate geographic location.

Wholesale distributor

Wholesaling includes all the activities involved in selling goods to those who buy for resale or for business use. The main function of the wholesale distributor is to balance supplies against retail requirements and to take the initiative of bringing produce from areas where it is plentiful and cheap to those where it is relatively scare and expensive. Wholesalers usually have a good knowledge of the market, access to the best information on trends and prospects and working capital to carry business risks as required.

Wholesalers usually obtain eggs from central wholesale markets, assembly merchants, collectors and local country markets; however, in some instances they go directly to the producers. Eggs may be purchased directly or accepted for sale on a commission basis. Many wholesalers have their own storage facilities. Wholesale distributors may engage specialized transport agencies to transport eggs or operate such services on their own account.

Central wholesale markets

Central wholesale markets receive shipments from large farms and from country markets, and constitute a supply source where wholesalers and retailers can obtain the various types of produce they need. General wholesale markets sell many different products, including eggs. Because it is the focus point of many smaller markets and also the point of contact for suppliers to important groups of consumers, a central market is usually the primary price-making mechanism for the production areas it serves. In this way it balances demand and supply.

Retailer

In urban areas, egg sales are made through retailers. Four types of retailers usually carry eggs in their shops:

- poultry shops where only eggs and poultry are sold;
- food shops specializing in eggs, poultry, cheese, butter, meat and fish;
- general food shops and supermarkets selling all kinds of foods and household goods; and
- meat markets where all types of meat are sold and eggs are also offered for sale.

In some instances retailers buy eggs directly from the producer and may have their own process-packing facilities.

As we have seen, marketing channels have different organizations that carry out different functions, or it may be possible that an organization carries out more than one function. Vertical integration occurs when more than one of the stages of the marketing channel is carried out by a single organization. For example, a wholesaler may have processing-packing facilities, retail outlets and employ collectors as well.

EVALUATION OF THE MARKETING CHANNEL

Before choosing a marketing channel or channels to market eggs, producers should carefully evaluate the following factors:

- market requirements and their ability to meet these;
- the type of intermediaries available;
- the number of intermediaries necessary to reach the market;
- alternative intermediaries different from the established marketing channel;
- the responsibilities of intermediaries and terms of possible agreements;
- costs involved;
- possible sales by the marketing channel; and
- the possibility of selling through a number of marketing channels.

Chapter 5
Pricing and sales policy

DEMAND AND SUPPLY

The level of demand for eggs is determined by the price, the number of potential consumers, their purchasing power and by the extent to which they prefer to buy eggs rather than alternative foodstuffs. From the point of view of supply, a price must be high enough to cover production, storage and transport costs. It is unlikely that suppliers will continue to supply eggs if the price remains below that required to cover their costs and give them at least as high a standard of living as they could obtain in other ways. Hence in the long run, market prices must be both low enough for consumers to purchase and high enough to ensure that producers will supply.

PRICING

Usually market demand and supply determine egg prices. It is important for producers to ascertain market prices for eggs and the price trends over a one-year period. Once market prices are known, producers will be able to calculate if that price or prices in a market or various markets will cover their costs and give them a sufficient profit. It must be remembered that prices change and that pricing information must be up to date when calculating possible profits. In some countries there are seasonal variations in both production and demand which affect the level of prices at various times of the year. These variations in prices should be noted by the producer in planning his/her production and marketing.

Producers must calculate both production costs and marketing costs.

Production costs

Refer to Chapter 1 for a detailed description of production costs. Tables 4 and 6 in that chapter are models that could be used for record keeping.

Marketing costs

Marketing costs will vary according to the method of marketing chosen (see Chapter 4). The main operating expenses for marketing include:

- packaging and storage;
- handling;
- transport;
- product losses;
- fees, taxes and unofficial payments, and
- unexpected costs.

Packaging and storage costs. Costs for packaging include the materials used for packaging, which may vary from a simple basket to a carton made of plastic, and labelling. The cost of storing the eggs must also be considered.

Handling costs. The cost of packaging the eggs, putting them into storage, loading them for transport and unloading them at their destination must all be calculated as handling costs. Each individual handling cost may not amount to much; however, the sum total of all such handling costs can be significant.

Transport costs. Costs for transport will vary according to the method of transport used and the distance covered.

Product losses. Produce can be lost during the marketing period. There are two types of losses – quality and quantity. Eggs exposed to heat with consequent deterioration is an example of quality loss. Breakage of eggs during transport on a bumpy road is an example of quantity loss.

Fees, taxes and unofficial payments. It may be that set fees have to be paid, for example, to a local authority for the use of a market stall. Taxes will have to be paid and, in some situations, bribes may be required to pass a roadblock or to access determined markets. These are all costs that must be considered.

Unexpected costs. It is always important to calculate expenses for unexpected events that may raise costs. For example, it could happen that a road is closed and this may result in a longer distance to be covered to consign eggs. This will raise costs.

In Table 9 we can see marketing costs in tabular form.

Table 9
Marketing costs

Costs	US$
Packaging/storage	
Handling	
Transport	
Product losses	
Fees, taxes, unofficial payment	
Unexpected costs	
Total costs	

The producer must calculate both production and marketing costs together as shown in Table 10.

At the end of the year, the producer can work out the production and marketing costs and the average market price for eggs over the year. After verifying how many eggs were sold during the year, the producer can calculate whether or not a profit was made.

Table 10
Total costs

Production costs	US$
Rearing (carried forward from Table 4)	
Houses	
Equipment	
Feed	
Labour	
Vaccinations	
Mortality	
Various expenses	
Total production costs	
Marketing costs	
Packaging/storage	
Handling	
Transport	
Product losses	
Fees, taxes, unofficial payments	
Unexpected costs	
Total marketing costs	
Total costs	

Price differences between markets

One way of checking pricing efficiency in a marketing system is to compare the prices of similar qualities and types of eggs in different markets. Where the differentials reflect the necessary cost of some essential marketing service such as transportation, the marketing system can be regarded as fairly efficient. In other cases, it may be found that these differentials are larger than might be expected. Poor reporting and communication of market news as well as bad transport and storage facilities are among the most common causes of such discrepancies.

It is normal for prices to be lower in production areas than in deficit centres of consumption. Sometimes, however, the differential is much larger than the transport and other marketing charges would warrant. Lack of market information may make it difficult for wholesalers to judge how much produce a market will absorb and to estimate accurately the quantities that are being brought in by other buyers. Lack of storage facilities may be another contributory factor. Storage facilities would enable the wholesalers to move eggs in and out of storage to correct imbalances of supply and demand. Frequently, transportation between production and consumption areas is expensive, difficult to organize and risks heavy losses. Provided there is competition between traders in these markets, such price differentials should contract as these defects are corrected.

Seasonal variations and cyclical movements

Seasonal changes in the prices of eggs mainly reflect variations in production. In temperate climates, the natural laying season is during the spring. Prices tend to be lower in the spring because of the plentiful supply and tend to be much higher in autumn when eggs are scarcer. In climates where seasonal changes are less marked, variations in the availability of feed often cause fluctuations in marketing supplies of eggs. Producers should plan to get the eggs to market when prices are high. An important consideration in adjusting to such cycles is not whether prices are high or low by any particular standard, but whether other producers decide to expand or cut down their breeding flocks in response to them. The main aim is to secure a more even supply of eggs over the year at relatively stable prices.

DEVELOPMENT OF SALES OUTLETS

Most producers and traders are interested in expanding their markets. The simplest approach is to dispatch a selected lot of eggs to some consumer centre where prices appear attractive and find out by experiment whether the net return is greater than that obtained locally. If this proves successful, other consignments of eggs may be sent. Before large consignments are prepared for distant markets, it is recommended that market potentials be investigated. By undertaking some marketing research, the risk of losses can be minimized and the chances of developing profitable trade relationships greatly increased.

Investigation of potential markets

In planning a sales development programme the following points merit careful attention:

- available supply;
- potential markets;
- controls; and
- type and quality of product.

Available supply. The number, type and quality of eggs possible to produce must be estimated realistically. A proportion of the eggs produced may not meet the quality standards desired. Seasonal and year-to-year variations in the supply are an important consideration.

Potential markets. Potential markets should be investigated by looking at the following criteria:

- eggs sales in markets where there is a deficit for eggs;
- price levels throughout the year;
- total sales level achieved;
- distribution and its costs;
- competition; and
- consumer likes and dislikes.

Controls. Each potential market may have control restrictions such as minimum quality standards as well as packaging and disease controls. These must be investigated accurately. Also, there may be informal restrictions on new producers who want to enter a market and these have to be verified.

Type and quality of produce. In a potential market the type and quality of eggs required for that market must be assessed carefully. Marketing research (see Chapter 6) can be used to determine the quality and form in which eggs are desired by consumers, and in what units and packaging they wish to buy them. Estimates of how much consumption would change and in what direction if a shift in income or price occurred could also be verified.

Selling arrangements

When a potential market has been located the next step is to establish trade contracts. It is important to select wisely the agent, distributor or retailer through which sales will be made. One must ascertain the reliability, contacts and facilities of the person or organization involved. Importantly, a contract should be stipulated that clearly defines the duties and obligations of all parties concerned and the duration of the agreement.

Chapter 6
Marketing services

Market information, marketing education and training, promotional campaigns to promote egg consumption, marketing research to aid in producer and trader decision making and the availability of credit are all needed to help a marketing system operate more efficiently. These activities may be seen as facilitating services for producers and traders. Marketing services include the following:

- Extension and training
- Market information services
- Marketing research
- Programmes to expand consumption
- Trade associations
- Credit

EXTENSION AND TRAINING

Those involved in production and marketing of eggs should engage regularly in training. The broad objectives of most egg marketing educational programmes are to help producers understand the demands of the market and modify their production and marketing accordingly. Processors/packers, wholesalers and retailers can be helped to become more effective and efficient so that eggs can be marketed with less waste, less loss in quality and at a lower cost.

Extension officers can lead meetings, discussions and demonstration programmes on egg production and marketing. They should make regular visits to production and marketing centres to keep in touch with current developments and problems. The extension officer can provide a valuable link between technical research workers and market intermediaries and the producers.

The duties of an extension officer are described below.

1. *Understand the functioning of the egg industry.* This involves looking at such issues as egg production processes, statistics, major enterprises, the geographic distribution of egg production, price trends, sales volumes, sales methods and when sales occur.

2. *Advise farmers on the possible potential of egg production.* Advice can be given on what marketing opportunities there may be, how to calculate the demand for eggs, how to calculate marketing and production costs and what processing and storage facilities may be required.

3. *Raw materials.* The extension worker must advise the farmers on where to obtain equipment and materials for building brooder and laying houses, feed, small chicks and all other materials that are necessary for production. Materials needed for packaging must also be considered. Importantly, the farmer must be advised on how to grow and manage small chicks, the feed required and the type of environment necessary. The input suppliers should be surveyed and their prices for equipment, small chicks, feed, etc., collected. Delivery and credit conditions with various suppliers should be covered. The extension worker should advise small farmers to group together to purchase and transport raw materials to the various small farms. This will result in cost savings for the farmers.

4. *Financing of raw materials.* Extension workers should determine how farmers could finance the required inputs. Can farmers rely on their own cash savings or credit institutions? If not, what credit is available and from which institutions, and is it possible to promote savings that may then be invested in egg production.

5. *Production.* The farmer needs to be advised on what breed to buy, when to buy day-old chicks, when to place grown chicks into the laying house, when they will start laying and how long they will lay profitably. The production cycle should be covered thoroughly and all requirements, such as feed, water, clean nests, etc., should be included.

6. *Post-production facilities.* Farmers should be advised on facilities that are required once eggs are produced, such as storage facilities, and cleaning, grading and packing facilities. Information concerning the cost of such facilities and where materials can be obtained should be provided.

7. *Promote small farmer associations.* Practical advice on the formation of cooperative or group production, packaging, processing and sales associations and pooling schemes should be given. Importantly, the extension worker should promote to farmers the idea of grouping or associating together. This will lead not only to savings in the purchase of inputs, but will also improve opportunities for egg marketing. The pool of raw materials, production and marketing capabilities will create a better bargaining position for small-scale farmers. It will also enable them to have better access to credit, and will give them the opportunity to adopt innovations more easily and at a lower cost.

8. *Understanding marketing.* Farmers must be assigned to understand what marketing is and what are the marketing channels for eggs. Different prices may be obtained from different markets. Farmers must be active in looking for buyers and in determining who they are, what price they may obtain and quantities of supply required and, furthermore, whether they pay in cash and when they pay, and whether the price they pay is higher or lower than that of other buyers. Farmers must learn how to calculate their production and marketing costs. They must also be able to understand when and where to sell eggs and the quantities to be sold based on market information. It is also important to understand the costs and possible profitability of storage.

9. *Pricing.* Farmers should be advised on the principal factors that form and influence prices. They should learn how to calculate costs and profit.

10. *Marketing channels.* Extension workers should constantly monitor the channels available. They should explain the channels, their efficiency and costs to farmers and advise on possible channel alternatives. Furthermore,

they should teach farmers how to monitor channels and explain the opportunities that may arise from using different channels and the relative cost savings that may be obtained.

11. *Legislation.* The extension workers should explain to the farmers the legislation that could affect production and marketing of eggs, relative quality standards, sales contracts, etc.

12. *Sources of market information.* Farmers should be told how to obtain market information from government, local municipalities, radio bulletins, etc. Farmers should be trained to carry out simple marketing research. (see section on marketing research below).

13. *Challenges and opportunities.* Possible risks and opportunities that may be present in the industry in months or years to come must be considered by the extension worker. They should advise on the need for smaller packaging, new production and processing techniques that may allow for cost savings, new market openings, etc.

14. *Requirements to improve marketing.* The extension worker should instruct farmers on a regular basis regarding the prevention of losses during handling and transport, standards, quality control, grading methods and candling, simple but effective cooling devices, etc.

15. *Visits.* Regular visits to packaging, grading and processing establishments should be made by the extension worker so that he can constantly monitor the situation. Where possible, extension workers should encourage farmers to visit production and processing facilities.

MARKET INFORMATION SERVICES

The importance of market information has to be emphasized. This information is of vital importance for producers and traders. It will enable them to produce and trade based on what markets require. Market information could be defined as a service, usually operated by the public sector, that involves the collection on a regular basis of information on prices, and in some cases quantity, of widely traded agricultural products from rural assembly markets, wholesale and retail markets. This service also involves the dissemination of this information on a timely and regular basis, through various media, such as radio and newspapers, to producers, traders and consumers.

Up-to-date reports on supplies available, quantities sold and in storage, prices paid at major markets at local, wholesale and retail levels are invaluable for an efficient marketing system. Marketing information services can help in the following ways.

- *Improve bargaining between producers and traders.*
- *Risk reduction.* Producers who have reliable and timely information, and who can interpret it, for example, can decide to which market they want to send their eggs in order to maximize returns. Information reduces transaction costs by reducing risks.
- *Identification of markets.* It is unlikely that producers and traders will consign eggs to a distant market unless they are reasonably confident of being able to sell at a profit. Market information can help in taking such a decision.
- *Allocation of productive resources.* Information on market price fluctuation over a period of time can help a producer decide whether to expand, contract or keep production constant. This information allows the producer to allocate production resources more efficiently.
- *Storage decisions.* Egg storage implies costs; therefore, producers and traders need to obtain a price that covers possible storage costs. Information on seasonal price trends is important for producers and traders.
- *Trade development.* Marketing information not only alerts producers to production possibilities, but can also give information on trading opportunities. This can lead to an increase in market outlets for the producers and make them more competitive.
- *Facilitating contractual agreements.* Contractual agreements between producers and traders usually carry a set price agreement for a period of time for the eggs supplied. Market information can help set a fair price in the contractual agreement and thus avoid disputes.

Assembling reliable, valid and unbiased reports is not an easy task. Experience in interpreting and checking information supplied by individual buyers and sellers is essential. The collection of market information is especially difficult when many transactions take place through private negotiations, yet it is here that it is most needed. Personal enquiries of buyer and seller may be necessary. The transactions covered should be those that have the most influence on price making and which concern the most important categories of eggs traded. Care should be taken to relate prices to quality, implying the use of a uniform set of specifications throughout the reporting sequence.

MARKETING RESEARCH

Marketing research is necessary in order to help producers make decisions regarding marketing. Marketing research can be defined as the systematic and objective search for, and analyses of, information relevant to the identification and solution of any problem in the field of marketing. Marketing research aids decision-making, however, it will not fully eliminate risk.

Marketing research has advantages and disadvantages. The main advantages of marketing research are:

- defining the needs and nature of customers and their ability and desire to buy;
- scanning the business environment;
- gathering needed information for decision-making;
- reducing risk;
- helping in production planning; and
- monitoring and controlling marketing activities.

Marketing research should be carefully planned and each step of the process analysed before the actual research begins. The first step is to clearly define the purpose of the research and the objectives. The objectives must be measurable, quantifiable and attainable. Costs of the research must be carefully evaluated and budgeted and the time duration considered.

Possible marketing research plan for eggs

1. *Recognition of information needed or problems.* It is important to define carefully the information that is required. For example, from a simple information requirement such as what eggs to sell, many sub-questions may arise such as the following.

   - What type of eggs is most in demand?
   - Are more brown eggs sold?
   - Are more white eggs sold?
   - What size egg is sold the most?
   - Do different outlets require eggs of different sizes, colour and packaging?
   - What is the market price?
   - Who is buying eggs?

2. *Definition of objective(s).* The objective or objectives of the research should be defined clearly. For example, do shopkeepers want eggs in trays or in retail cartons?

3. *Deciding on what tool(s) to use to gather information.* Information may be gathered by observation, survey, or from already published and available data. Observation is simply observing phenomena and recording them as they occur, for example, observing consumers at a market and what they buy. A survey involves questioning consumers, wholesalers and retailers in order to gain information of interest. A survey also involves preparing a questionnaire. For example, consumers may be asked what type of eggs they prefer, while retailers could be asked what type of eggs they sell the most.

4. *Formulation of appropriate tool(s).* Importantly, if either observation or survey is chosen as a tool to collect information, the tool must be carefully designed. The design for observation should tell the observer if he or she must look at a particular aspect of a market or observe the whole market. The design for the survey should look at what type of questions should be

asked and how they should be asked. For example, the questions could be as follows.

- Do you like eggs? Yes/No
- Do you buy eggs? Yes/No
- Do you buy eggs every day? Yes/No
- Do you buy eggs at least once a week? Yes/No

5. *Information gathering.* When the information is being gathered, it must be done in an unbiased and uniform manner and be recorded accurately.

6. *Analysis of information.* Once the information has been gathered, it must be analysed and evaluated. For example, if consumer data has been gathered regarding egg buying habits, it is necessary to group the various results into categories, such as income and/or geographic location of customers.

7. *Results and conclusions.* The summarized data will give some clear results from which conclusions may be drawn. For example, if it was found that the majority of consumers eat brown medium-sized eggs, one should aim to produce brown medium-sized eggs.

PROGRAMMES TO EXPAND CONSUMPTION
The main methods that can be used to expand consumption are improved marketing organization and consumer education and promotion.

Improved marketing organization
Improvements in marketing organization and methods are often a prerequisite to expanding consumption and hence production. The existence of well-run buying, packaging/processing and distribution enterprises promotes both production and consumption. It dispels doubts in the minds of potential consumers regarding quality, freshness and wholesomeness of the eggs offered.

Consumer education and promotion

A continuous programme of consumer education and promotion may help increase egg consumption. Eggs are of high nutritional value, easily digestible and especially good for children, pregnant women and the elderly. Educating young school children regarding the goodness of eggs may prove over time to be a good strategy to increase consumption. Radio advertising, radio talk shows, advertising, collaboration with public and private agencies seeking to improve health, living and nutritional standards may all increase consumption. Such programmes can be carried out by single enterprises or enterprises grouped together in order to share the costs and benefits of the initiative. Importantly, such initiatives should be carried out in collaboration with retail outlets, schools, hotels, restaurants and hospitals so as to obtain the maximum benefit of the educational and promotional campaign.

TRADE ASSOCIATIONS

It may be of great value to form a trade association for egg producers. An association can impose determined standards and requirements in order to guarantee that eggs produced by its members are of a determined quality. The association may help in introducing and disseminating knowledge and new techniques of production and marketing. It may put producers into good bargaining positions *vis-à-vis* transport facilities, wholesalers and retailers.

Trade associations are set up on a voluntary basis by enterprises and are usually most effective when organized by individuals and enterprises with common business interests. Membership is voluntary and funds are obtained either as a fixed amount per year from each member or as a fixed amount on volume sold. Usually officers are elected to perform association duties and permanent or *ad hoc* committees may be appointed to handle certain issues or programmes.

CREDIT

Producers' credit needs have an important bearing on marketing organization and costs. Limited access to credit is a common barrier to the establishment of improvements and increased production and marketing. For example, if the establishment of new production facilities such as hen houses is required, the producer may need to obtain credit.

In order to acquire eggs and finance their movement through marketing channels, traders must either draw the necessary capital from their own resources or be able to obtain it on short-term loan.

Marketing success in Chile

The Chilean egg industry is predominately based on the traditional family business. The industry has about 8 million layers in production on an annual basis. Two million layers are found in large production facilities, while the greater part, 6 million layers, comes from small-scale producers.

In Chile, between 75 and 80 percent of all eggs marketed are white shell eggs, the remaining are brown. Ninety-two percent of egg sales are through public markets and small retail stores, while the remaining 8 percent are sold in supermarkets.

About 80 percent of egg producers are associated with Asohuevo, Chile's producer association. This association carries out strong publicity campaigns and managed to increase per capita consumption from 105 eggs in the 1980s to 165 in the 1990s.

Chapter 7
Live bird marketing

Layers start a second year of egg production usually after 71 to 78 weeks of age; however, the eggs produced are inferior in number and quality to those produced in the first year. The birds should be culled at the end of their first year of production and sold for meat. As discussed in Chapter 1, a producer may have up to a maximum of four different age flocks present at one time on the farm, which indicates that culled birds are sold on an occasional basis. The sale of culled birds provides extra income to the producer.

In the tropics and in dry areas, slaughtered layer meat deteriorates very quickly if refrigeration is not available. For this reason, layer meat is purchased either live or just slaughtered. Unless carcasses can be chilled rapidly and kept below a temperature of 4° C, they should be sold within a few hours after slaughter.

QUALITY CRITERIA
Composition and attributes of layer meat
Weight is a determinant characteristic in the marketing of live birds. The type of feed, the breed of the bird and how it has been treated will define the weight of each layer. The main constituents of layer meat are water, protein, and fat. Increases in collagen and elastin, the proteins forming the connective muscle tissues, are related to the toughness of the meat of layer birds.

Variations in the amount of deposited fat are associated with quality. The age and sex of a bird influence the fat content, as does a high caloric diet.

Layer meat provides a good source of high quality protein, iron and phosphates and the B vitamins riboflavin and niacin. The vitamin content of the meat is influenced to a very large degree by the vitamin content of the feed consumed.

Eating quality

Meat varies in acceptability to consumers according to its tenderness, juiciness and flavour when cooked. Age and sex are the primary characteristics distinguished in commercial poultry handling. Broilers, which are birds reared specifically for meat, can be marketed from the age of 8 weeks up to 20 weeks. Birds under 12 weeks of age, of either sex, have very tender meat. Birds between 12 and 16 weeks of age, of either sex, also have relatively tender meat and can be cooked by roasting. Birds that are marketed between 16 and 20 weeks have meat that is less tender but which can also be cooked by roasting. The meat of mature layers (over 20 weeks old at the time of culling) is less tender than that of a roaster and therefore is best cooked by steaming or simmering in water.

Appearance

Layer birds must be sound, healthy, clean and fit for human consumption. The birds must have a healthy appearance. Missing or displaced feathers, bare skin in evidence and broken bones or cuts detract from the appearance of a carcass. If the bird is not in good condition, the consumer will not buy the bird even though it has been slaughtered, as the carcass will show the defects.

Measures to prevent deterioration during marketing

In tropical and dry climates, the most common form of marketing poultry meat is to sell the birds live. The quality of birds is affected greatly by the methods employed in transporting them from the farm. Considerable death losses, broken wings and legs, and bruises result if birds are handled roughly or carried in unsuitable or overcrowded containers.

Live birds must be transported in a manner that allows for plenty of air ventilation to protect the birds from heat. Birds should be transported in crates, constructed so that the birds' legs cannot pass through the bars yet air can circulate easily. Crates of wire netting on a wood frame are safe, light in weight, and suitable for handling and transport. The entrance of the crate should be easy to open and close and centrally situated so that all parts of the crate are within reach.

When birds are being caught for marketing, they should be caught with a crook as shown below.

Catching birds

Source: Smith, 1990

The bird should be approached from behind, the crook should be placed just above the foot and the bird picked up gently with care. Under tropical and subtropical conditions, this operation should be carried out at the end of the day in dim light or darkness, when the birds are more docile. Once caught, the birds should be placed in the crate as seen below.

Placing birds in a crate

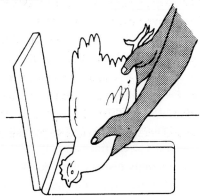

Source: Smith, 1990

The bird should be lowered gently into the crate, head first, the wings held close to the body with one hand, with the other hand gently holding the legs. Overcrowding in each crate must be avoided. For example, a crate that has dimensions of 80 × 60 × 30 cm will hold a maximum of ten birds. Crates must be handled with great care and fastened safely when they are loaded onto transport vehicles. Transport must take place during the cooler part of the day in order to avoid the birds being exposed to sunlight and heat. They must not be shaken or jolted excessively when being transported and the time spent travelling must not be excessive. Weight losses ranging from one to three percent during transport from farm to market or processing plant are common.

Marketing slaughtered birds

Birds to be marketed should be fasted before being slaughtered. If birds are fed mash, they should be fasted four to six hours before slaughter; if fed grain, ten hours of fasting will be required. But if feed and water are withheld from the birds for fourteen hours or longer, there is a high risk of the guts breaking during slaughter, which would enable organisms such as salmonella to infect the meat, the slaughtering tools and the slaughtering area during processing.

When refrigeration is available it is possible to market the birds in the following manner:

- dressed (slaughtered, bled and plucked);
- eviscerated/ready to cook (the carcass minus head and feet but including liver, heart, and the gizzard less its contents and lining);
- poultry parts (legs, thighs, wings, breast, back, neck and giblets); and
- boned (muscle, fat and skin only).

The rate of quality deterioration or spoilage depends very much on the form in which the carcass is marketed. A bird with only feathers and blood removed will spoil much more slowly than eviscerated, cut-up or boned carcasses. Spoilage bacteria are confined largely to the intestinal tract and skin. These organisms are rapidly dispersed in the tissues of eviscerated, cut-up or boned carcasses and there are few or no natural defences to prevent their multiplication. The cold temperatures found in refrigeration slow down contamination.

Grading and standardization

Grading of live poultry is generally informal. Buyers note the breed, age, weight and general condition of the birds on offer. Because the feathers obscure the proportion of flesh to bones, they usually catch a few birds and feel the breasts to see how much meat they carry. Price negotiations will then proceed on the basis of market price. Broad standards, such as weight, appearance and ease in processing, are used to distinguish first and second quality grades, but essentially this is difficult and subjective.

Formal standards and grades can be adapted more easily to carcasses because the quality features can be seen more clearly. The following factors are usually considered:

- *conformation* (the shape of the carcass);
- *fleshing* (leg, wing and breast muscles are full and well developed, assuring a good proportion of meat to bone);
- *fat* (fat under skin is important because it gives the carcass a pleasing light appearance by covering up the pink or red muscles underneath);
- *skin dislocations, tears* and *cuts*; and
- *bruises*.

All these features are appraised in relation to species, sex and age.

Conditions for standardized grading

The feasibility of applying uniform quality standards depends very much on how birds are marketed. Because of the difficulty of classifying live birds by more than broad age, sex and type categories, standardized grading in most countries relates only to the marketing of birds already in carcass form. Consumer interest in standardized grading is also related closely to the form in which the bird is sold. If the consumers can see and handle the live birds, they are able to form their own conclusions regarding quality. The greater the degree of processing undertaken during marketing the more difficult this becomes. Age and condition are difficult to judge in cut-up and packaged meat and a grade label becomes the buyers' main guide. Trading must be on a constant and large scale if grading is to be undertaken systematically and accurately. Ease in the adoption of uniform grading procedures is also related to the degree of standardization that has been reached in the production process.

Where substantial quantities of meat are wholesaled and retailed as carcasses, and proper refrigeration is available during handling and marketing, there are many advantages in standardized grading. For example, transactions between distant markets can take place without personal inspection by the buyer.

PROCESSING

The degree of processing undergone during marketing varies greatly both between and within countries. It depends primarily on the form in which the consumer wishes to take delivery of the bird and, secondly, on the equipment available to enterprises and distributors. Some consumers buy live birds and slaughter them when needed, particularly if refrigeration is not available. Many consumers do not want to kill the birds themselves, however, they may wish to see the birds alive before buying them. This is very important in areas where production is not specialized. In these areas sellers usually hold stocks of live birds in cages so that consumers can see them. Once a sale has been made, the seller slaughters and dresses the bird according to consumer desires.

A bird can be slaughtered by dislocating its neck or by cutting its throat. The blood must be completely drained out and then the feathers can be plucked. Dry plucking involves plucking feathers by hand when the body is still warm. Usually four to ten birds can be plucked per hour. Once feathers have been removed the carcass can be prepared accordingly: dressed, eviscerated/ready to cook, poultry parts or boned.

In countries where consumers prefer ready-to-cook birds and refrigeration is widely available for processing, transportation, selling and storing, mechanized processing is widely used (see Photograph 32).

MARKETING ORGANIZATION FOR LIVE BIRDS

It is important to gather information first to see if there is a market for culled birds. Sales would be on an occasional basis, therefore, it is advisable to ascertain whether consumers and retailers would want to buy live birds at such irregular intervals. Producers usually have a marketing system developed to sell eggs and it may be possible to sell culled birds using the same system. Direct marketing includes door-to-door sales, street hawking, selling at a producer's local market and selling to local retailers.

Some consumers prefer to have the birds slaughtered after they have inspected them alive. This would involve learning how to slaughter and pluck birds properly. An easy and practical method to slaughter live birds at a customer's home, on the street or at a producer's market would be necessary. Provision must be made for transportation of the birds in cages. A larger vehicle may be required so the cages can be transported along with the eggs. When transporting live birds and eggs together it is important that the quality of eggs does not deteriorate because of bird manure.

A careful evaluation of the costs involved and the income obtained from the direct sale of live birds must be made to see if this method of marketing is worthwhile. Furthermore, the time spent by the producer attending to clients, slaughtering birds and cleaning up after the slaughter must be taken into consideration.

Farm-gate sales also involve slaughtering the birds for the consumers. It is important to know how to slaughter a bird and how to pluck and prepare the carcass. It is necessary to buy proper utensils and to have a location where the birds can be slaughtered. Before slaughtering, the birds must be checked for disease and other problems such as cuts, broken bones, etc. The slaughtering and processing procedures shown below must be carried out in a covered area that is well ventilated and clean. All utensils and equipment used for slaughtering must be kept clean.

Slaughtering. Birds can be slaughtered by dislocation of the neck, cutting of the jugular vein, stunning and cutting, piercing of the brain and decapitation. The most common used are dislocation of the neck, cutting the jugular vein and stunning.

- *Neck dislocation.* The bird has to be held by its feet. The neck must be pulled downwards and then bent sharply backwards. Considerable force is required to break the neck.
- *Cutting of jugular vein.* The bird must be held by the feet and an incision has to be made in the jugular vein just under the head of the bird at the beginning of the neck.
- *Stunning.* Birds are stunned with an electric stunner applying 90 V for one-half a second and then the jugular vein is cut. Stunning will keep the bird from struggling.

Bleeding. All the blood must be removed from the bird. This can be done by placing the slaughtered bird in a bleeding cone or holding the bird above a bucket for one and one-half to two minutes. For hygienic reasons it is important that the blood is not allowed to spread in the slaughtering areas.

Plucking. Dry plucking consists of removing the feathers from the bird when it is still warm by hand or by machine. Scalding makes plucking easier. It involves placing the bird in hot water (between 50° and 55° C) for about two minutes and then plucking the feathers by hand or machine. A common plucking machine has two drums with rubber fingers that revolve in opposite directions pulling the feathers off the body in a downward motion.

Evisceration. At this point the bird can be processed to fit the consumers' requirements. The carcasses can be dressed, boned and cut into pieces. The feet, head, neck and giblets, heart, liver and gizzard can be removed. Careful attention must be paid not to break or cut the intestines of the bird because this would release many harmful organisms into the meat.

Chilling. (This is possible only where refrigeration is available.) Before chilling, the meat and the giblets have to be washed thoroughly and left to drain. The meat and giblets can be chilled in cold water, slush ice, crushed ice or solid carbon dioxide. To chill to the optimum cold storage temperature of between 2° and 4° C will take about 45 minutes.

Packaging. The selection of materials for packaging depends on needs such as physical strength, permeability to water vapour and other gases, transparency, cold resistance and heat sealing properties. The bird can be packed with the giblets, which are packed in a clean plastic bag and placed inside the bird or packed separately. The carcass can be placed in a plastic bag, from which as much air as possible has been drawn, and firmly sealed.

Storage. Meat can be kept for seven days at a temperature of 2° C; however, if storage is required for a longer period it is best to store at a temperature of − 5° C or even to − 18° C.

Collectors, who regularly visit production facilities to collect eggs, may be interested in buying the culled hens. Processor-packers, wholesalers and retailers may also be interested. Alternatively, producers can market the culled birds separately from existing egg marketing arrangements. They will have to determine whether it is more feasible to market the birds directly or to use channel members for their marketing. The producer will have to evaluate costs against income obtained from the sale of birds. For example, a producer could dispatch the entire lot of birds to an abattoir, where they would be slaughtered, processed and packed. This may be feasible in terms of costs and income. Yet, alternatively there could be a higher income in selling the birds separately at a local producers' market. South African egg producers sell their culled birds to entrepreneurs who run spent hen depots, and who in turn may sell them to street hawkers.

References

Belayavin, C.G. & Wells, R.G. 1987. *Egg quality - current problems and recent advances.* Sevenoaks, UK, Butterworths.

Crosby, T.N. 1981. *Food packaging materials.* London, Applied Science Publishers Ltd.

Daghir, N.J. 1995. *Poultry production in hot climates.* Wallingford, UK, CAB International, 1995.

Fellows, P. & Axel, B. 1993. *Appropriate food packaging.* Geneva, Tool Publications for the ILO.

FAO. 1961. *Marketing eggs and poultry*, by J.C. Abbott, J.C. & G.F. Stewart. Marketing Guide No. 4, Rome.

FAO. 1977. *Keeping chickens.* Be tter Farming Series, Rome.

FAO. 1988. *Egg and poultry marketing, India,* by F.J. Jensen & S.C. Jackson. Field document. Rome.

FAO. 1989. *Indian egg marketing ... out of shell ... and growing*, by R. Balasubramanian. Asian Livestock Series, Rome.

FAO. 1992. *Small-scale poultry processing*, by D. Silverside & M. Jones, AGA, Rome.

FAO. 1992. *Costs, margins and returns in agricultural marketing*, by L.D. Smith. Marketing and Agribusiness Development Paper No. 1. Rome.

FAO. 1993. *Prospects of poultry meat and egg production in Eastern Europe,* by K.D. Flock & K. Meyn. Report. Rome.

FAO. 1993. *A guide to marketing costs and how to calculate them*, by A.W. Shepherd, AGS. Rome.

FAO. 1994. Working paper on poultry raising/egg production, Balochistan Province, Pakistan, by M. Kane, Field document. Rome.

FAO. 1997. *Agricultural and food marketing management*, by I.M. Crawford, AGS Marketing and Agribusiness Text, Vol. 2. Rome.

FAO. 1997. *Marketing research and information systems*, by I.M. Crawford, AGS Marketing and Agribusiness Text, Vol. 4. Rome.

FAO. 1997. *Market information services - theory and practice,* by A.W. Shepherd, FAO Agricultural Services Bulletin No. 125. Rome.

FAO. 1998. *Poultry meat and egg production, Northern Atoll Region, Maldives,* Terminal Statement Report. Rome.

FAO. 1998. *Village chicken production systems in Africa,* by A.J. Kitalyi, AGA. Rome.

FAO & European Bank for Reconstruction and Development. 1999. *Poultry/eggs and poultry meat,* Agribusiness Handbooks, Vol. 6. Rome.

Holland, B., Unwin, D.I. & Bus, D.H. 1989. *Milk products and eggs. The composition of foods.* Surrey, UK, Unwin Brothers Ltd.

Hunton, P. 1995. *Poultry production,* World Animal Science, No. 9. Amsterdam, Elsevier.

Kekeocha, C.C. 1985. *Poultry production handbook.* London, Macmillan Publishers Ltd.

Kohls, R.L. & Uhl, J.N. 1985. *Marketing of agricultural products,* 6th edition. New York, Macmillan.

Larbier, M. & Leclecq, P. 1992. *Nutrition and feeding of poultry.* Loughborough, UK, Nottingham University Press.

Mead, G.C. & Wells, R.G. 1999. *Poultry meat science.* Wallingford, UK, CAB International Publishing.

Mead, G.C. 1989. *Processing of poultry.* London, Elsevier.

Oluyemi, J.A. & Roberts, F.A. 1979. *Poultry production in warm wet climates.* London, Macmillan Publishers, Ltd.

Paine F.A. & Paine, H.Y. 1983. *A handbook of food packaging.* Glasgow, UK, Leonard Hill.

Panda, B. & Mohaptra, S.C. 1989. *Poultry production.* New Delhi, Indian Council of Agricultural Research.

Pesti, G.M. & Reid, W.M. 1992. *Raising healthy poultry under primitive conditions.* Seattle, Washington, Christian Veterinary Mission.

Prabakaran, R. 1998. *Commercial chicken production.* Chennai, India, P. Saranaya.

Sacharow, S. & Griffin, R.C. 1980. *Principles of food packaging,* 2nd edition. Westport, CT, AVI.

Sim, S.J. & Nakai, S. 1994. *Egg uses and processing technologies, new developments.* Wallingford, UK, CAB International.

Smith, A.J. & Leclecq, P. 1990. *Poultry.* London, Macmillan Publishers Ltd.

Stadelman, W.J. & Cotterill, O.T. 1986. *Egg science and technology,* 3rd edition. Westport, CT, AVI.

Van Eekeren, N. & Mass, A. 1990. *Small scale poultry production in the tropics,* Wageningen, Netherlands, CTA.

On the web

Danish Poultry Network. www.poultry.kvl.dk

Poultry Information Network. www.wattnet.com

International Egg Commission. www.internationalegg.com

Egg – Nutrition Centre. www.enc-online.org

American Egg Board. www.aeb.org

United States Department of Agriculture, Agricultural marketing services. www.ams.usda.gov

Canadian Egg Marketing Agency. www.canadaegg.ca

British Egg Information Service (BEIS). www.britegg.co.uk

University of Minnesota. www.extension.umn.edu

University of Missouri – Columbia. www.asrc.agri.missouri.edu/poultry/index.htm

University of Nebraska – Lincoln. www.ianr.unl.edu/pubs/poultry

Photographs

1-5	Examples of laying houses	107, 108
6	Ideal egg shape	109
7	Degrees of spotting and blood diffusion in eggs	109
8	Effects of temperature and storage on eggs	110
9	Holding eggs while candling	110
10	Appearance of various qualities of eggs in candling	111
11-14	Candling – various egg quality deficiencies	112, 113
15	Abnormal egg shape	113
16	Eggs packed in baskets with straw	114
17	Basket packing	114
18	Fillers	115
19	Plastic transparent fillers	115
20	Small cases made of paperboard or wood pulp holding six eggs	116
21	Small cases made of transparent plastic holding six eggs	116
22	Intensive egg production with egg conveyor belt	117
23	Egg stacking	117
24	Candling machine	117
25	Hand packing eggs	118
26	Eggs arriving at weighing and packing machine	118
27	Weighing and packing machines for predetermined egg weights	119
28	Weighing and packing machine	119
29	Eggs ready for transport	120
30	Street sales	120
31	Eggs for sale in a producers' market	120
32	Mechanized processing	121
33	Selling live birds at a market	121

1-5. **Examples of laying houses**

Courtesy www.poultry.kvl.dk

Examples of laying houses, continued

6. **Ideal egg shape**

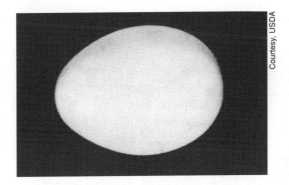

Courtesy, USDA

7. **Degrees of spotting and blood diffusion in eggs**

Courtesy, USDA

8. **Effects of temperature and storage on eggs**

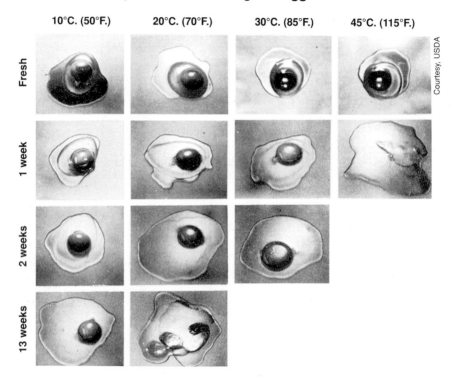

Courtesy, USDA

9. **Holding eggs while candling**

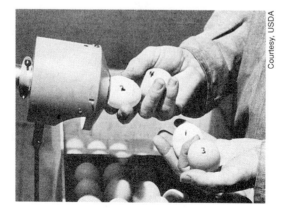

Courtesy, USDA

10. **Appearance of various qualities of eggs in candling**

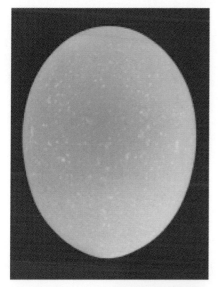

AA Quality – Yolk outline slightly defined

A Quality – Yolk outline fairly well defined

B Quality – Yolk outline plainly visible

Courtesy, USDA

11-14. Candling - various egg quality deficiencies

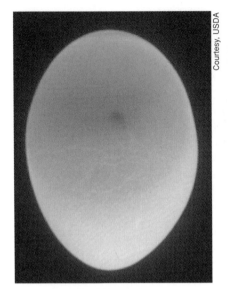

Small blood spot

Bloody white

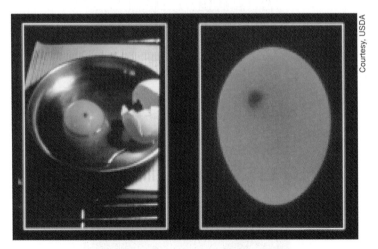

Candled and broken-out appearance of a large blood spot

Candling - various egg quality deficiencies, continued

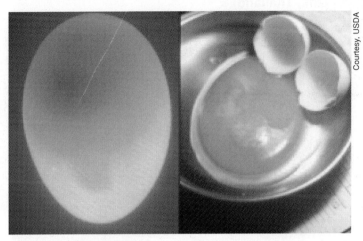

Candled and broken-out appearance of a mixed rot

15. Abnormal egg shape

16. Eggs packed in baskets with straw (Bangkok, Thailand)

17. Basket packing (Bangkok, Thailand)

18. **Fillers**

19. **Plastic transparent fillers**

20. Small cases made of paperboard or wood pulp holding six eggs

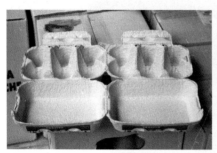

E. Seidler

21. Small cases made of transparent plastic holding six eggs

E. Seidler

22. Intensive egg production with egg conveyor belt

E. Seidler

23. Egg stacking

24. Candling machine

E. Seidler

E. Seidler

E. Seidler

25. **Hand packing eggs**

E. Seidler

26. **Eggs arriving at weighing and packing machine**

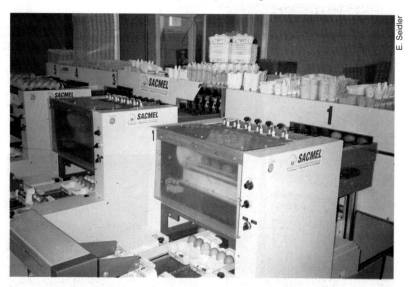

E. Seidler

27. Weighing and packing machines for predetermined egg weights

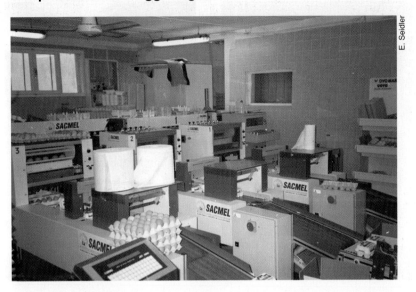

E. Seidler

28. Weighing and packing machine

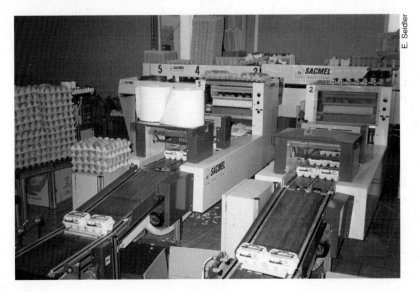

E. Seidler

29. **Eggs ready for transport** 30. **Street sales**

31. **Eggs for sale in a producers' market**

32. **Mechanized processing**

E. Seidler

33. **Selling live birds at a market**

E. Seidler

FAO TECHNICAL PAPERS

FA0 AGRICULTURAL SERVICES BULLETINS

1	Farm planning in the early stages of development, 1968 (E F S)
2	Planning for action in agricultural development, 1969 (E F S)
3	Karakul processing, 1969 (E)
4	Bread from composite flour, 1969 (E* F S)
5	Sun-drying of fruits and vegetables, 1969 (E F S)
6	Cashew nut processing, 1969 (E F S)
7	Technology for the production of protein foods from cottonseed flour, 1971 (E F S)
8	Cassava processing, 1971 (New edition, 1977, available in E, F and S in the FAO Plant Production and Protection Series, No. 3)
9	Worldwide list of food technology institutions, 1971 (E/F/S*)
10	Technology of production of edible flours and protein products from groundnuts, 1971 (E F S)
11	Technology of production of edible flours and protein products from soybean, 1971 (E F S)
12	A guide for instructors in organizing and conducting agricultural engineering training courses, 1971 (E F S)
12 Sup. 1	Elements of agricultural machinery, Vol. 1, 1977 (E S)
12 Sup. 2	Elements of agricultural machinery, Vol. 2, 1977 (E S)
13	Fruit juice processing, 1973 (E S)
14	Environmental aspects of natural resource management – agriculture and soils, 1972 (E F S)
15	Manual on sericulture:
	Vol. I – Mulberry cultivation, 1976 (E F)
	Vol. 2 – Silkworm rearing, 1973 (E F)
	Vol. 3 – Silk reeling, 1972 (E F)
16	The use of aircraft in agriculture, 1972 (New edition, 1974, available in E, F and S in the FAO Agriculture Series, No. 2)
17	Airtight grain storage, 1973 (E F S)
18	Rice testing methods and equipment, 1973 (C E)
19	Cold storage – design and operation, 1973 (E F S)
19/2	Design and operation of cold stores in developing countries, 1984 (Ar E F S)
20	Processing of natural rubber, 1973 (E)
21 Rev. 1	Agricultural residues: world directory of institutions, 1978 (E/F/S)
21 Rev. 2	Agricultural residues: world directory of institutions, 1982 (E/F/S)
22	Rice milling equipment operation and maintenance, 1974 (C E)
23	Number not assigned
24	Worldwide list of textile research institutes, 1974 (E/F/S)

25	Molasses utilization, 1975 (E F S)
26	Tea processing, 1974 (E)
27	Some aspects of earth-moving machines as used in agriculture, 1975 (E)
28	Mechanization of irrigated crop production, 1977 (E)
29	Non-mulberry silks, 1979 (E)
30	Machinery servicing organizations, 1977 (E)
31	Rice-husk conversion to energy, 1978 (E)
32	Animal blood processing and utilization, 1982 (C E S)
33	Agricultural residues: compendium of technologies, 1978 (E/F/S)
33 Rev. 1	Agricultural residues: compendium of technologies, 1982 (E/F/S)
34	Farm management data collection and analysis, 1977 (E F S)
35	Bibliography of agricultural residues, 1978 (E/F/S)
36	China: rural processing technology, 1979 (E)
37	Illustrated glossary of rice-processing machines, 1979 (Multil)
38	Pesticide application equipment and techniques, 1979 (E)
39	Small-scale cane sugar processing and residue utilization, 1980 (E F S)
40	On-farm maize drying and storage in the humid tropics, 1980 (C E)
41	Farm management research for small farmer development, 1980 (C E F S)
42	China: sericulture, 1980 (E)
43	Food loss prevention in perishable crops, 1981 (E F S)
44	Replacement parts for agricultural machinery, 1981 (E F)
45	Agricultural mechanization in development: guidelines for strategy formulation, 1981 (E F)
46	Energy cropping versus food production, 1981 (E F S)
47	Agricultural residues: bibliography 1975-81 and quantitative survey, 1982 (E/F/S)
48	Plastic greenhouses for warm climates, 1982 (E)
49	China: grain storage structures, 1982 (E)
50	China: post-harvest grain technology, 1982 (E)
51	The private marketing entrepreneur and rural development, 1982 (E F S)
52	Aeration of grain in subtropical climates, 1982 (E)
53	Processing and storage of foodgrains by rural families, 1983 (E F S)
54	Biomass energy profiles, 1983 (E F)
55	Handling, grading and disposal of wool, 1983 (Ar E F S)
56	Rice parboiling, 1984 (E F)
57	Market information services, 1983 (E F S)
58	Marketing improvement in the developing world, 1984 (E)
59	Traditional post-harvest technology of perishable tropical staples, 1984 (E F S)

60	The retting of jute, 1985 (E F)
61	Producer-gas technology for rural applications, 1985 (E F)
62	Standardized designs for grain stores in hot dry climates, 1985 (E F)
63	Farm management glossary, 1985 (E/F/S)
64	Manual on the establishment, operation and management of cereal banks, 1985 (E F)
65	Farm management input to rural financial systems development, 1985 (E F S)
66	Construction of cribs for drying and storage of maize, 1985 (E F)
67	Hides and skins improvement in developing countries, 1985 (C E F)
68	Tropical and sub-tropical apiculture, 1986 (E)
68/2	Honeybee mites and their control – a selected annotated bibliography, 1986 (E)
68/3	Control de calida de la miel y la cera, 1990 (S)
68/4	Beekeeping in Asia, 1986 (E)
68/5	Honeybee diseases and enemies in Asia: a practical guide, 1987 (E)
68/6	Beekeeping in Africa, 1990 (E)
69	Construction and operation of small solid-wall bins, 1987 (E)
70	Paddy drying manual, 1987 (E)
71	Agricultural engineering in development: guidelines for establishment of village workshops, 1988 (C E F)
72/2	Agricultural engineering in development – The organization and management of replacement parts for agricultural machinery, Vol. 2, 1988 (E)
73/1	Mulberry cultivation, 1988 (E)
73/2	Silkworm rearing, 1988 (E)
73/3	Silkworm egg production, 1989 (E)
73/4	Silkworm diseases, 1991 (E)
74	Agricultural engineering in development: warehouse technique, 1989 (E F S)
75	Rural use of lignocellulosic residues, 1989 (E)
76	Horticultural marketing – a resource and training manual for extension officers, 1989 (E F S)
77	Economics of animal by-products utilization, 1989 (E)
78	Crop insurance, 1989 (E S)
79	Handbook of rural technology for the processing of animal by-products, 1989 (E)
80	Sericulture training manual, 1990 (E)
81	Elaboración de aceitunas de mesa, 1991 (S)
82	Agricultural engineering in development: design and construction guidelines for village stores, 1990 (E F S)
83	Agricultural engineering in development: tillage for crop production

in areas of low rainfall, 1990 (E)

84   Agricultural engineering in development: selection of mechanization inputs, 1990 (E F S)

85   Agricultural engineering in development: guidelines for mechanization systems and machinery rehabilitation programmes, 1990 (E)

86   Strategies for crop insurance planning, 1991 (E S)

87   Guide pour l'établissement, les opérations et la gestion des banques de céréales, 1991 (F)

88/1   Agricultural engineering in development – Basi blacksmithing: a training manual, 1992 (E S)

88/2   Agricultural engineering in development – Intermediate blacksmithing: a training manual, 1992 (E F S)

88/3   Agricultural engineering in development – Advanced blacksmithing: a training manual, 1991 (E F S)

89   Post-harvest and processing technologies of African staple foods: a technical compendium, 1991 (E)

90   Wholesale markets – Planning and design manual, 1991 (E)

91   Agricultural engineering in development: guidelines for rebuilding replacement parts and assemblies, 1992 (E S)

92   Agricultural engineering in development: human resource development – training and education programmes, 1992 (E F S)

93   Agricultural engineering in development: post-harvest operations and management of foodgrains, 1994 (E F S)

94   Minor oil crops:
Part I – Edible oils
Part II – Non-edible oils
Part III – Essential oils, 1992 (E)

95   Biogas processes for sustainable development, 1992 (E F)

96   Small-scale processing of microbial pesticides, 1992 (E)

97   Technology of production of edible flours and protein products from soybeans, 1992 (E F)

98   Small-, medium- and large-scale starch processing, 1992 (E F)

99/1   Agricultural engineering in development: mechanization strategy formulation – Vol. 1, Concepts and principles, 1992 (E F S)

100   Glossary of terms for agricultural insurance and rural finance, 1992 (E F S)

101   Date palm products, 1993 (E)

102   Experiencias de mercadeo de pequeños agricultores en el marco de proyectos de desarrollo rural integrado, 1992 (S)

103   Banking for the environment, 1993 (E S)

104   Agricultural engineering in development: agricultural tyres, 1993 (E)

105   Apicultura práctica en América Latina, (S)

106   Promoting private sector involvement in agricultural marketing in

Africa, 1993 (E F)

107   La comercialización de alimentos en los grandes centros urbanos de América Latina, 1993 (S)

108   Plant tissue culture: an alternative for production of useful metabolites, 1993 (E)

109   Grain storage techniques – Evolution and trends in developing countries, 1994 (E F)

110   Testing and evaluation of agricultural machinery and equipment – Principles and practices, 1994 (E F S)

111   Low-cost, urban food distribution systems in Latin America, 1994 (E S)

112/1   Pesticide application equipment for use in agriculture – Vol. 1, Manually carried equipment, 1994 (E F)

112/2   Pesticide application equipment for use in agriculture – Vol. 2, Mechanically powered equipment, 1995 (E F S)

113   Maintenance and operation of bulk grain stores, 1994 (E)

114   Seed marketing, 1994 (E)

115   La selección, prueba y evaluación de maquínas y equipos agrícolas, 1995 (E F S)

116   Safeguarding deposits – Learning from experience, 1995 (E)

117   Quality assurance for small-scale rural food industries, 1995 (E)

118   Pollination of cultivated plants in the tropics, 1995 (E)

119   Fruit and vegetable processing, 1995 (E)

120   Inventory credit – An approach to developing agricultural markets, 1995 (E S)

121   Retail markets planning guide, 1995 (E F)

122   Harvesting of textile animal fibres, 1995 (E)

123   Hides and skins for the tanning industry, 1995 (E)

124   Value-added products from beekeeping, 1996 (E)

125   Market information services – Theory and practice, 2001 (E F S)

126   Strategic grain reserves – Guidelines for their establishment, management and operation, 1997 (E)

127   Guidelines for small-scale fruit and vegetable processors, 1997 (E)

128   Renewable biological systems for alternative sustainable energy production, 1997 (E)

129   Credit guarantees – An assessment of the state of knowledge and new avenues of research, 1998 (E)

130   L'étude des SADA des villes dans les pays en développement – Guide méthodologique et opérationnel,1998 (F)

131   Les SADA des villes, 1998 (F)

132   Aliments dans les villes – Collection d'ouvrage 1, 1998 (F)

133   Aliments dans les villes – Collection d'ouvrage 2, 1998 (F)

134   Fermented fruits and vegetables – A global perspective, 1998 (E)

135   Export crop liberalization in Africa – A review, 1999 (E)